MW00650032

Enjoy your new club wines

Wade

My Mother Leslie and Me - Harvest 2009

This book is dedicated to the Kunde family; to the 1st generation who had the courage and foresight to come to this country and settle in the beautiful Sonoma Valley, to the 2nd generation who continued to develop the vineyard land, and to the 3rd generation who had the business savvy and work ethic to expand on the land and vineyards that are part of our enterprise to this day. Most importantly, this book is dedicated to my Mom, a wonderful, strong and caring woman who believed in the strength of family and was always my biggest fan.

KUNDE *Style*
Family, Food & Wine

Welcome to the Club!

by Marcia Kunde Mickelson

A Note of Thanks

To Jim, my wonderful husband of 35 years who makes me smile every day and inspires me to be the best I can be. To my beautiful children, Bobby and Jamie, who make me proud in all that they have accomplished in their young lives. And, last but not least, to our dedicated team at Kunde Family Winery who make things happen on a daily basis — from their creativity, passion, and dedication, to their continued pursuit of perfection.

ISBN-13-978-0-692-04355-4

FIRST EDITION

Photography by Timm Eubanks
Food Styling by Joanna Badano
Book Design by Nelson Sobel Design

Other photography:
Vieraphotographics (pg. 6 lower left); Alyssa Groff (pg. 28, center and pg. 126, lower left); Nat & Cody (pg. 29); Jessamyn Harris (pg. 48 upper left), Lindsey Tatum Photography (pg. 77 upper left); Brenda Hawkes (pg. 77 lower left); Darwin Bell (pg. 106 top).

Contents

There are a lot of places to live, work, and play in this world. The Kunde family is fortunate to have been brought up in northern California wine country where the beauty of the land is a central part of our lifestyle. Daily routines follow the rhythm and seasonality of the vineyards, which in turn guide the creation of our wines. The winery is a constant sea of action and along the way we get to share our little slice of heaven with the multitude of guests who visit us from near and far.

This is where our story begins…in Sonoma Valley with my great grandfather Louis Kunde's purchase of the Wildwood Vineyards ranch in Glen Ellen, 1904. His inspired land acquisition laid the groundwork for a century plus legacy of land stewardship and sustainability that still resonates today with the 4th and 5th generations. Louis' artistic winemaking style quickly led his wines to be highly sought after, serving as a testament to his cunning business mind and creativity. Upon his passing in 1922, his legacy was handed over to his son, Arthur "Big Boy" Kunde, followed by Bob and Fred Kunde, who continued to work the land and expanded upon the original ranch footprint to what is now an 1,850 acre contiguous estate. The 5 million year-old iron rich volcanic red soils continue to bless our wines every vintage, while yielding to the whims of mother nature.

Growing up I remember my Dad heading off into the vineyards with my brothers in tow to cultivate the vines—nipping, tucking, plowing, pruning and harvesting. I was lucky to spend time at home with my Mom who inspired me to become a gracious hostess, creative cook and a life-long animal lover. My mother taught me how to entertain with ease and grace as I watched her whip up a tasty meal at a moment's notice when my Dad would bring in last minute cattle or vineyard clients. My folks shared their love of the land with so many, and they always enjoyed a hearty meal served with a bottle of great wine, surrounded by friends and family.

Today my life revolves around the hustle and bustle of winery activities, our growing family with the addition of two grandchildren (our 6th generation), and our dynamic Hereford cattle operation. I love to entertain, much in the same way as my Mom did with last minute guests and friends stopping by.

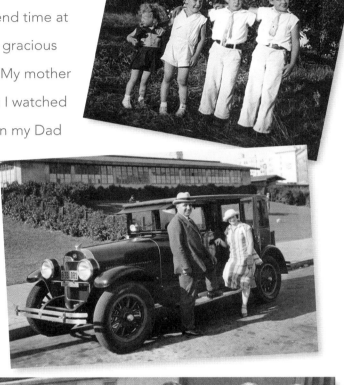

2nd and 3rd Generation Kunde Family

3rd generation family members Leslie, Bob, Jane, Richard, Fred and Sis

We continue to be surrounded by the beauty of the Kunde Estate and derive unparalleled bliss that comes from nurturing the next generation. I hope you delight in the breathtaking images that we've featured and savor the delectable family recipes that we've shared throughout the four seasons in wine country. Cheers to living life well and to wonderful family, great food and delicious Kunde wines.

Original Kinnybrook barn stucture where the Tasting Room stands today

Marcia Mickelson

Marcia Kunde Mickelson
4th Generation Winegrower
Chief Operating Officer
Kunde Family Winery

Winery groundbreaking Spring 1990

You don't
scare me big
boys!

Spring

Verdant rows paint the hillsides, fields of mustard dance
in the crisp air, and bright orange wild calendula tuck
in between the dormant vines — each decorating the
springtime landscape and awaiting the first signs of
life coming back to the slumbering vines. Then, with a
flourish, from the warmth of the spring sunshine, the
vines begin their seasonal rebirth. First with the swelling
of a bud, soon followed by the emergence of a miniscule
leaf, tender to the kiss of an early morning frost. The
springtime vineyard awakens.

Oysters on the Half Shell with Magnolia Lane Mignonette

Created by Katy Long, wife of Kunde Winemaker Zach Long.

Ingredients:

1 dozen fresh oysters – cleaned and opened

4 T red wine vinegar

4 T seasoned rice vinegar

1/2 shallot – peeled and finely minced

1/2 red jalapeño – seeded and finely minced

2 T Kunde Magnolia Lane Sauvignon Blanc

Fresh cracked pepper to taste

Sliced lemons for garnish

Preparation:

Prepare the oysters and place on a serving dish. Mix the remaining ingredients together and spoon onto each half-shelled oyster. Serve sliced lemons alongside for an additional garnish. **Serves 2-3.**

Serve with:

Kunde Family Winery Magnolia Lane Sauvignon Blanc

"My favorite oysters are Miyagis and Kumamotos. They tend to be small but they are so tasty!"

Tip:
Want to get fancy?
Serve over a bed
of crushed ice for a
beautiful presentation.

Olive Tapenade served with Baked Brie Cheese and Crostini

Sitting around a warm fire pit is the perfect atmosphere to enjoy this delightful appetizer.

Ingredients:

1 sourdough baguette – thinly sliced

1/2 cup olive oil – divided

1 cup Kalamata olives – pitted

1 T capers – rinsed and drained

2 anchovy fillets in olive oil – drained

1 garlic clove

1/4 cup fresh basil leaves

1/4 cup fresh Italian parsley leaves

1 T lemon juice

1 tsp lemon zest

1/4 tsp chili flakes

6-8 oz Brie cheese round – triple crème

Preparation:

Preheat oven to 425 degrees. Place sliced sourdough on a foil covered baking sheet and brush the bread with a small amount of olive oil. Bake 8-10 minutes until lightly toasted. Remove from oven and cool.

For the tapenade, place olives, capers, anchovies, garlic, herbs, 1/4 cup olive oil, lemon juice, lemon zest and chili flakes into a Cuisinart. Pulse until desired chunkiness, should be well blended. Taste as you may need to add more lemon juice.

Place Brie round on sheet pan lined with parchment paper. Bake under low broiler for 2-4 minutes until the top is golden. Serve with olive tapenade and crostini. **Serves 6-8.**

Serve with:
Kunde Family Winery Chardonnay

"The combination of warm melted Brie with the Kalamata olives is hard to resist."

Shrimp Crostini with Fresh Dill

Fresh shrimp and dill – two of my favorites! A perfect appetizer to serve at a cocktail party.

Ingredients:

1 sourdough baguette – thinly sliced

Olive oil

8 oz package cream cheese – softened

1/2 cup mayonnaise

2 T Dijon mustard

1 1/4 lbs cooked small shrimp – coarsely chopped

1/2 cup green onions – minced

1 1/2 T fresh dill – chopped

1 T lemon juice – freshly squeezed

1 tsp lemon peel – grated

1 tsp tobasco

Salt and pepper

Small sprigs of fresh dill for garnish

Preparation:

Preheat oven to 425 degrees. Place sliced sourdough on a foil covered baking sheet and brush the bread with a small amount of olive oil. Bake 8-10 minutes until lightly toasted. Remove from oven and cool.

Beat together cream cheese, mayonnaise and Dijon mustard in large bowl. Fold in shrimp, green onions, dill, lemon juice, lemon peel and tobasco. Season with salt and pepper to taste.

Spread 1 T shrimp mixture on top of each toasted baguette slice. Broil briefly until the shrimp mixture just begins to brown, about 1-2 minutes. Top with a small fresh sprig of dill. **Serves 8-10.**

Serve with:

Kunde Family Winery Sauvignon Blanc – Block 4SB20

Tip:

Short on time? Buy pre-packaged crostini. Not as good as fresh but your company will be so happy with the shrimp and dill that it won't matter!

Fresh Fava Bean Bruschetta

If you can't find fresh fava beans, check your local farmer's market. The color of the beans in this recipe is just stunning.

Ingredients:

1 sourdough baguette – thinly sliced

Olive oil

1 1/2 lbs fresh fava beans – cleaned, blanched and drained

2 T preserved lemon – thinly sliced and chopped (can substitute lemon zest)

1-2 T fresh lemon juice

2 T fresh mint – chiffonade

Salt and pepper

8 oz ricotta cheese (Bellwether Farms is my choice)

Preparation:

Preheat oven to 425 degrees. Place sliced sourdough on a foil covered baking sheet and brush the bread with a small amount of olive oil. Bake 8-10 minutes until lightly toasted. Remove from oven and cool.

Prepare fava beans and place in bowl. With a fork, smash about 1/2 of them and leave the rest whole, halved or in pieces. Add preserved lemon, lemon juice, mint, 1 T olive oil, pinch of salt and pepper and mix together. Adjust the olive oil and lemon juice to your desired taste.

To serve, spread ricotta cheese on each crostini and spoon on the desired amount of fava bean spread. Serve immediately. **Serves 4-6.**

Serve with:

Kunde Family Winery Viognier

Asian Chicken Wings with Shredded Cabbage Slaw

Packed with flavor, these wings are definitely a crowd-pleaser!

Ingredients:

2 lbs chicken wings

Marinade:

2 T olive oil

1/4 cup honey

2 T soy sauce

1 T ginger – minced

1-2 tsp garlic chili sauce – depending on how spicy you prefer

2 garlic cloves – minced

1 T seasoned rice vinegar

2 tsp orange or tangerine zest

2 T orange or tangerine juice

Cabbage Slaw:

3 cups Napa cabbage – shredded

1 cucumber – thinly sliced

1 carrot – shredded

2 scallions – thinly sliced

1/2 cup cilantro – chopped

1/2 cup roasted peanuts – chopped

Dressing:

1/4 cup soy sauce

1/4 cup seasoned rice vinegar

1 T maple syrup

1 T toasted sesame oil

Preparation:

In a small bowl, combine all ingredients for the marinade. Place chicken wings in glass bowl and cover with marinade. Marinate for 30 minutes or up to 2 hours in refrigerator, covered. While chicken marinates, make the cabbage slaw. Combine the slaw ingredients and mix together in a large bowl. In a separate bowl, whisk all dressing ingredients. Set both bowls aside.

Preheat oven to 400 degrees. Place chicken wings on parchment-lined baking sheet, reserving marinade and cooking wings for 15-20 minutes until charred a bit, turning occasionally. While wings are cooking, pour reserved marinade in a sauce pan over medium heat and reduce until thickened. Brush sauce over cooked wings.

Arrange wings on a platter with slaw that has been tossed with a portion of the dressing, reserving some in a side bowl for dipping the wings. Garnish with sesame seeds, scallions and chopped peanuts if desired. **Serves 6 to 8.**

Serve with:

Kunde Family Winery Chardonnay

Red Grapefruit and Avocado Salad

The bright citrus combines beautifully with the creamy avocado for a delightful springtime salad.

Ingredients:

1 small head of butter lettuce – separated and cleaned

1 medium grapefruit – cut, peel, remove pith, slice into 1/4 inch rounds and then into halves or quarters

1 avocado – peeled and cut into small wedges

1 small fennel bulb – thinly sliced

2 cups of pea shoots or baby sprouts

Sprigs of mint for garnish

Green Goddess Dressing:

1/2 cup regular plain yogurt – if using Greek yogurt, you may need to thin with a few T's of water

1 avocado – peeled and scooped out

1/4 cup parsley

1/4 cup mint

1 garlic clove

2 T olive oil

1 T champagne vinegar

2 T lemon juice

1 tsp honey

1/2 cup water

Salt and pepper

Preparation:

Put all dressing ingredients in blender and process until smooth. Check for desired taste and consistency, may need to add a touch more salt or lemon juice.

Arrange butter lettuce on platter in whole or torn leaves. Add the grapefruit, avocado, fennel and pea shoots and arrange. Drizzle dressing over salad or serve in a dish and let each person drizzle their own. Garnish with sprigs of mint. Dressing will store in refrigerator 3-5 days. **Serves 4-6.**

Serve with:

Kunde Family Winery Sauvignon Blanc – Block 4SB20

"I cook by taste so I always make sure to try the dressing before serving. A little adjustment of salt and pepper or lemon juice can make a huge difference!"

Seafood Capellini Salad

This is a wonderful side dish salad or can be served as a light main entree.

Ingredients:

1 package capellini pasta

1 1/4 lbs small fresh shrimp – divided

1 bunch green onions – sliced

1 red bell pepper – chopped fine

3 stalks celery – chopped fine

1/2 bunch parsley – chopped fine

2 cloves garlic – minced

1/2-3/4 cup olive oil

1/4 cup red wine vinegar

Salt and pepper

Endive spears

Preparation:

Cook pasta according to package directions. Rinse with cold water, drain and toss with a small amount of olive oil to prevent sticking. Once the pasta is cool, toss with 1 lb shrimp and remaining ingredients, excluding the endive and 1/4 lb of shrimp for garnish. Taste and add a bit more vinegar or salt and pepper to your liking. Place endive spears on plate and spoon a generous helping of pasta on top. Pile the extra shrimp on top for a pretty presentation. **Serves 3-4.**

Serve with:

Kunde Family Winery Chardonnay – C.S. Ridge Vineyard

"The combination of capellini and shrimp with the vinegar is tangy and very refreshing."

Chinese Chicken Salad with Napa Cabbage and Toasted Sesame Seeds

This easy to prepare salad is a go-to of mine when the days get a bit warmer. Sitting on the patio with a glass of Chardonnay—it's a salad that I just can't put down!

Ingredients:

4 skinless, boneless chicken breasts

3 T low sodium soy sauce

1/2 head iceberg or romaine lettuce – chopped

1/2 head Napa cabbage – chopped

1 1/2 cups dried chow mein noodles

3 medium carrots – grated

11 oz can mandarin orange segments – drained

1 bunch green onion – sliced thin

1 medium red bell pepper – diced

1/2 cup roasted peanuts – chopped

Toasted white sesame seeds

Dressing:

1 cup mayonnaise

1 cup fresh cilantro leaves

3 T seasoned rice vinegar

2 T toasted sesame oil

3 T low sodium soy sauce

1 T sugar

1 T fresh ginger – minced

Pinch of cayenne pepper
(more if you like a bit more heat)

Preparation:

Place chicken breasts in a medium sauce pan, cover with water, add soy sauce and bring to a boil. Cover the pot, turn off heat and let sit for 30 minutes. Remove chicken from pot and let cool. Cut into bite size pieces.

To prepare the dressing, place all ingredients in a blender and process until smooth in texture.

Place all remaining ingredients except for sesame seeds in a large bowl. Add chicken pieces and dress the salad, mixing well to incorporate the flavors. Sprinkle sesame seeds over the salad.
Serves 3-4.

Serve with:
Kunde Family Winery Chardonnay

Asian Flank Steak Salad

Easy to prepare and full of flavor. Great salad to pair with white or red wine.

Ingredients:

1-1 1/2 lbs flank steak – set out at room temperature

1 cup savoy cabbage – finely shredded

1 cup cilantro – chopped

1 cup mint – chopped

1 carrot – thinly shredded

1/2 English cucumber – thinly sliced

1 watermelon radish – thinly sliced into matchsticks

2-3 handfuls baby arugula

4-6 oz thin brown rice noodles

1/2 cup roasted peanuts – chopped, for garnish

Dressing:

2 T ponzu sauce or soy sauce

3 T sesame oil

1/4 cup fresh lime juice

1 1/2 T fish sauce

1 tsp chili garlic paste

2 tsp lime zest

1-2 T honey

1/4 cup olive oil

Preparation:

Combine all dressing ingredients in small bowl except olive oil. Slowly whisk in the olive oil to emulsify.

On a sheet pan, place flank steak and drizzle 1 T of dressing and 1 T of additional olive oil. Let rest 30 minutes to 1 hour. Boil rice noodles according to package directions and toss with 1 T dressing. Set aside in large bowl.

Heat grill or grill pan on high heat. Oil grill and grill meat 6-8 minutes per side or until desired doneness (internal temperature is 135 degrees for medium rare). Let rest 5-10 minutes. Slice thinly and diagonally against the grain.

To serve, add all vegetables and herbs to the rice noodles and toss with more dressing to desired taste. Arrange meat on salad, sprinkle with peanuts and serve. **Serves 4-6.**

Serve with:
Kunde Family Winery Red Dirt Red

Grilled Portobello Sandwich with Caramelized Onions, Pesto Mayo and Balsamic Glaze

A yummy vegetarian alternative to a classic hamburger.

Ingredients:

4 fresh Portobello mushroom caps – you can remove the gills with a spoon or leave them

Olive oil

1 large sweet yellow onion – sliced thin into 1/2 moons

Salt and pepper

1/2 cup mayonnaise

2-3 tsp fresh or prepared pesto

1 red pepper – roasted, peeled, seeded and cut into 1/2 inch strips

4 focaccia sandwich rolls

4 slices provolone cheese

1 cup arugula

Balsamic Glaze:

1/2 cup balsamic vinegar

1 T honey

Preparation:

To prepare the balsamic glaze, combine the balsamic vinegar and honey in a saucepan over medium low heat for about 20 minutes or until thickened. Set aside.

Brush the mushrooms with olive oil and place on a sheet pan. In a skillet over medium heat, add 1-2 T olive oil. When hot, add sliced onion, salt and pepper and cook until caramelized, about 15-20 minutes. Set aside. In a small bowl, combine the mayonnaise and pesto. Cover and place in refrigerator until ready to use.

Prepare roasted pepper on a grill or char on a gas stove top. Cook until skin is thickened and blistered all over. Transfer pepper to a small bowl and cover tightly with plastic wrap for about 10-15 minutes. Take pepper out of bowl, remove skin, seeds, ribs, slice and place back in bowl. Cook mushrooms on a medium grill turning until heated through, about 5-7 minutes. Set aside. Toast the buns on the grill and transfer to a platter.

To assemble sandwich, spread each set of the rolls with 2 T of pesto mayonnaise. Add a grilled mushroom cap, cheese, onion, roasted pepper and arugula. Drizzle with the balsamic glaze followed by the top roll. Serves 4.

Serve with:
Kunde Family Winery Merlot

Looking mischievous

Wolfhounds on parade

Lamb Chop lollipops

Linguini with Fresh Baby Clams in a Chardonnay Infused White Sauce

This creamy garlic and Chardonnay sauce just sings with the linguini and clams. Delizioso!

Ingredients:

1 box dried linguini pasta

3 cloves fresh garlic – crushed

6 T olive oil

1 T flour

1/2 cup Chardonnay

1/4 cup fresh Italian parsley – finely chopped

1/2 tsp dried oregano leaves

3, 6.5 oz cans minced clams

Salt and pepper

1 1/2 lbs baby clams in their shells – pre-steamed and opened

Romano cheese – freshly grated

Sliced lemons

Preparation:

Cook the pasta in boiling, salted water until al dente or to your liking. At the same time, sauté the garlic in the olive oil over low heat until golden, but not brown. Stir in the flour until a smooth paste is formed. Gradually add the Chardonnay, parsley and oregano, stirring constantly until the sauce is thickened and smooth. Add the 3 cans of minced clams with their liquid, salt and pepper to taste. Cook until heated through.

Plate the pasta and then ladle the sauce over the cooked linguini. Tuck in the steamed clams, add more sauce and sprinkle all with freshly grated Romano cheese. Serve with sliced lemons as a garnish. Serves 4-6.

Serve with:
Kunde Family Winery Chardonnay – Wildwood Vineyard

Tip:
When purchasing fresh clams in their shell, do not seal the bag as they need to breathe before cooking. If clams do not open when steamed, discard.

Teriyaki Chicken with Savoy Cabbage and Scallions

Sweet and savory, this simple chicken bowl makes for a great lunch or dinner.

Ingredients:

1/3 cup mirin rice wine

1/2 cup soy sauce

3-4 T honey – depending upon desired sweetness

4-6 boneless, skinless chicken thighs

2 cloves garlic – crushed

1 small savoy cabbage – thinly sliced

2-3 cups cooked brown or white rice

2 scallions – thinly sliced

2 T toasted sesame seeds

Preparation:

In small sauce pan over low heat, combine mirin, soy sauce, honey and cook until slightly thick, about 20 minutes. Remove from the heat and let the sauce cool (it will thicken more as it cools). Place chicken thighs in a dish and brush both sides with 1-2 T of the sauce, then rub with garlic cloves. Let sit for 20 minutes. Meanwhile slice the cabbage and sauté over medium heat until slightly wilted. Set aside in bowl. Heat grill or grill pan on medium high heat. When hot, cook thighs 7-10 minutes turning occasionally until done. Place on cutting board to rest, then slice into 1/2 inch strips.

In individual serving bowls, place rice on the bottom followed by the cabbage. Then add chicken and drizzle with sauce. Garnish with the sliced scallions and toasted sesame seeds. Serve with extra sauce alongside. Serve immediately. **Serves 4-6.**

Serve with:

Kunde Family Winery Chardonnay – C.S. Ridge Vineyard

Chicken Saltimbocca with Prosciutto and Fresh Sage

One of my husband's favorites! Prosciutto and fresh sage make this an exceptionally tasty and beautiful dish.

Ingredients:

1/2 cup flour

Salt and pepper

4 boneless, skinless chicken breast halves

8 fresh sage leaves

4 slices prosciutto

Olive oil

3/4 cup dry vermouth

2-3 tsp Meyer lemon juice – freshly squeezed

4 T butter – cut into 4 pieces

1 T fresh Italian parsley – minced

Preparation:

Preheat oven to 350 degrees. Combine flour and 1 tsp salt and 1 T pepper in a shallow bowl. Pat chicken breasts dry and dredge in the flour mixture, shaking off any excess. Lay the breasts flat and top with 2 sage leaves. Wrap 1 slice of prosciutto around each breast, pressing slightly to adhere.

Set a wire rack on a rimmed baking sheet to hold the breasts. Heat 2 T olive oil in a large skillet over medium heat. Add two of the chicken breasts to the heated pan, top side down, and cook until golden brown, about 3 minutes. Turn the breasts over, being careful not to dislodge the sage and prosciutto, and cook the second side until golden brown as well, about 3 more minutes. Place the cooked breasts on the wire rack, tent with foil to keep warm, and cook the remaining two breasts in the same manner. Place the breasts in the oven for approximately 25 minutes, or until the chicken is cooked thoroughly and no longer pink on the inside.

While chicken is cooking, prepare the sauce. Over medium heat, stir the vermouth into the pan, scraping up the browned bits, and simmer until reduced to about 1/2 cup, 5-7 minutes. Stir in the fresh lemon juice. Reduce heat to low and whisk in the butter, one slice at a time. Turn off heat and stir in the fresh parsley. Season with salt and pepper to taste. Check for tartness as you may want to add more lemon juice. Spoon sauce over the cooked chicken breasts. This chicken is also very nice served over a bed of long grain and wild rice pilaf. **Serves 4-6.**

Serve with:
Kunde Family Winery Reserve Chardonnay

Grilled Lamb Chops with Pistachio Herb Sauce

The blend of pistachios and herbs really brings out the flavor in the chops.

Ingredients:

8-10 lamb chops

Salt and pepper

Lamb Marinade:

1/4 cup olive oil

1 T fresh rosemary – minced

2 tsp fresh thyme – minced

4 garlic cloves – minced

2 tsp Dijon mustard

Pistachio Herb Sauce:

1/4 cup pistachios

1 small garlic clove

1 cup fresh parsley

1/2 cup fresh mint

1-2 T lemon juice

1/2 cup olive oil

Salt and pepper

Preparation:

Prepare the lamb marinade first. In a small bowl, combine olive oil, herbs, garlic and Dijon mustard. Place lamb chops on a sheet pan and season with salt and pepper. Spoon marinade over lamb chops making sure to coat both sides well. Let sit for at least 30 minutes or even overnight in the refrigerator. Be sure to remove from refrigerator at least 30-45 minutes before grilling.

Prepare the Pistachio Herb Sauce while the lamb is marinating. Place all sauce ingredients in a food processor and process until well blended. Taste and adjust if necessary with salt, pepper and lemon juice.

When grill is hot, cook lamb chops about 3-5 minutes per side for medium rare or until desired doneness. Let rest 5 minutes, then serve with Pistachio Herb Sauce. **Serves 4.**

Serve with:

Kunde Family Winery Zinfandel – Heritage Block

"These chops are like eating adult lollipops – using your hands is a must!"

Pork Satay with Cucumber Lettuce Wraps and Zesty Peanut Sauce

A perfect tapas or light dinner to enjoy with friends on the patio.

Ingredients:

1 lb pork tenderloin – cut into 1/4 inch thick strips

Olive oil

Peanut Sauce:

1/3 cup peanut butter

1/2 cup canned coconut milk

1 small piece of fresh ginger

1 small piece of fresh turmeric

2 tsp sriracha sauce – more or less depending on desired spiciness

2 T lime juice – freshly squeezed

1 T soy sauce

1 T fish sauce

1 T honey

Plate Presentation:

10-12 lettuce cups (butter lettuce works well)

2 radishes – thinly sliced

1/2 English cucumber - thinly sliced into rounds

1 scallion – thinly sliced

Cilantro and mint sprigs for garnish

1/2 cup peanuts – chopped

Toasted sesame seeds

Tip:
Make sure to presoak the skewers otherwise your springtime soirée might become a springtime flambé!

Preparation:

To begin, make the peanut sauce. Put all ingredients for the sauce in a blender and blend until smooth.

Marinate the pork in a 1/4 cup of sauce, cover and place in refrigerator for at least 30 minutes. Set aside remaining sauce. After pork has marinated and the skewers have been soaked in water for at least 30 minutes, thread the pork onto the skewers. Pre-heat barbecue or grill pan over medium heat. Brush grill or pan with oil and when ready, cook pork, turning occasionally until cooked through, about 8-10 minutes.

To serve, arrange skewers on a platter with lettuce cups, radishes, cucumber, scallions, cilantro, mint sprigs, chopped peanuts and serve with remaining peanut sauce. Remove pork from skewer, place in lettuce cup and top with remaining ingredients. **Serves 4-6.**

Serve with:

Kunde Family Winery Reserve Chardonnay

Asian Noodle Salad with Fresh Mango and Beef Filet

A tasty Asian inspired dish that marries bright herb flavors with ripe mango and beef filet.

Ingredients:

1 package Chinese noodles

1 1/2 cups cherry tomatoes – halved

1 1/2 cups mango – peeled and cubed

1 cup Napa cabbage – shredded

1 cup cilantro leaves – chopped

1 cup mint leaves – chopped

1 cup basil leaves – chopped

2 scallions – sliced thinly

Salt and pepper

1 lb beef filet

1/2 cup roasted peanuts – chopped, for garnish

1 T sesame seeds – garnish

Lime Drizzle:

3 T lime juice

Zest of 1 lime

1-2 garlic cloves – minced

1/2 tsp ginger – grated

3 T soy sauce

1 T honey

2 T toasted sesame oil

1/3 cup olive oil

Salt and pepper

Preparation:

Prepare the Lime Drizzle first. Put all ingredients for the lime drizzle in a blender and blend until smooth. Taste and adjust seasoning if necessary.

Cook noodles according to directions on package. Rinse, drain and set aside to cool in a serving bowl. Drizzle with a little olive oil to prevent sticking. Prepare all remaining fresh ingredients, excluding the filet, and set aside in another bowl. Save a little bit of cilantro, mint and basil for garnish.

Preheat grill on high for 10 minutes. Season the filet with olive oil, salt and pepper then grill until desired doneness, 7-8 minutes. Let rest, slice and cut into bite size chunks.

To assemble salad, toss noodles with drizzle. Add vegetables, herbs, meat and toss to combine. Check for flavor and add more drizzle and salt and pepper if needed. Garnish with chopped peanuts, cilantro, mint, basil and sesame seeds. Serve immediately. **Serves 4-6.**

Serve with:
Kunde Family Winery Zinfandel

Strawberry Balsamic Tartlets

Simple, beautiful and delectable!

Ingredients:

2 baskets strawberries – cleaned and sliced

1 T sugar

1 tsp balsamic vinegar

1/2 vanilla bean scraped or 1/4 tsp vanilla

Salt

8 oz mascarpone

2 tsp honey

1 package puff pastry – thawed according to package directions

Egg wash or cream to brush puff pastry

Mint sprigs for garnish

Preparation:

Mix strawberries with sugar, balsamic vinegar, vanilla and a pinch of salt in a glass bowl and let macerate for 1/2 hour. In a separate bowl, mix mascarpone with honey until well incorporated.

Preheat oven to 400 degrees. Unfold sheet of puff pastry onto a baking sheet lined with parchment and cut the puff pastry into 6 squares. With a sharp knife, lightly score the dough 1/2 inch from edges, creating a border. Try not to cut through the dough. Brush the border with egg wash or cream and sprinkle with sugar. Freeze or refrigerate for 10 minutes and then bake until golden, about 12-15 minutes. Let cool and then gently press center to flatten and create a bowl.

To assemble tartlets, spoon a dollop of mascarpone mixture into each shell and top with the macerated strawberries. Serve with a drizzle of the juice from the strawberries and a sprig of mint if desired. Serve immediately. **Serves 6.**

Serve with:
Kunde Family Winery Summer's Blush Rosé

"You'll be asking yourself how such an elegant dessert is so easy to make!"

Springtime Strawberry Pie

This is the first dessert I make each spring when I see it's fresh strawberry season. My friend Caryn shared this recipe from her Mom. Scrumptious!

Ingredients:

Pillsbury pie crust

3 baskets of strawberries – washed and sliced

1 cup water

2 T cornstarch

3 drops red food coloring

Granulated sugar to taste

3 1/2 oz cream cheese – room temperature

1/2 cup powdered sugar

1/2 tsp vanilla

1/2 pint fresh whipped cream

Mint sprigs for garnish

Preparation:

Bake pie crust according to package directions and set aside to cool.

Mash 1/2 of strawberries in a saucepan. Add water, cornstarch and food coloring. Bring to a rolling boil until thickened. Let cool. Add remaining strawberries to cooked berry mixture and dust with sugar to taste.

In a separate bowl, mix cream cheese with powdered sugar and vanilla. Once creamy, fold in whipped cream. Spread filling into the baked pie shell. Top the cream cheese mixture with the strawberry mixture. Place in refrigerator and let chill until ready to serve.
You can decorate the top with fanned strawberry slices and a sprig of mint if desired. **Serves 6-8.**

Serve with:
Kunde Family Winery 1904 Dessert Cuvée

Tip:
I use Pillsbury brand pie dough for a nice, light crust. It's also a great time saver.

Leslie's Wine Cake

This was one of my Mom's favorite go-to desserts when time was limited and guests were on their way. A simple sweet treat! Even better with a little scoop of vanilla ice cream or whipped cream.

Ingredients:

1 pkg yellow cake mix

1 (4 1/2 oz.) pkg vanilla instant pudding mix

4 eggs

3/4 cup vegetable oil

3/4 cup dry sherry

1 tsp nutmeg

Powdered sugar

Preparation:

Preheat oven to 350 degrees. In a large bowl, combine all of the ingredients, except for the powdered sugar. Mix with electric mixer for 3 minutes at medium speed. Pour batter into greased bundt cake pan. Bake for approximately 45 minutes or until tested done and toothpick comes out clean. Cool in pan for about 5 minutes before turning out on rack. Once cool, sprinkle lightly with powdered sugar. Serves 8-10.

Serve with:

Kunde Family Winery Sweet Leslie

"This is a very simple dessert. With the flavors of vanilla, nutmeg and sherry, it's a perfect cake to pair with a rich dessert wine."

Tip:
Make sure to heavily grease your bundt pan. This cake is so yummy the pan might not want to give it up!

Ready for Easter!

C'mon Teddy!

Jordan 5th generation

Let's take a hike!

Spring babies meet!

Summer

June, July and August bring the glow of summer—balmy long days, beautiful sunsets, and glorious evenings. The vines luxuriate in the warmth of the atmosphere as they send their tendrils and canopy of leaves towards the rays of the sun. The winery bustles as the tourist season begins in earnest, filling our patio tasting areas with joyful revelers tasting the newest vintages and releases. The cellar crews concentrate on bottling the last of the prior two year's vintages as they wait with anticipation for the upcoming harvest. Patio parties, afternoon soirées, and poolside dining all create a festive atmosphere as we savor summertime fare and the bounty of our glorious gardens.

Uncle Dick's Sangria

My Uncle Dick would make this delicious Sangria for all of his summer parties. This festive concoction is really delicious (and potent!) and especially fun for a backyard gathering.

Ingredients:

3 oranges – sliced into wedges

1 good sized bunch red grapes

1/2 pineapple – sliced

2 grapefruits – sliced into wedges

1 papaya – sliced

3 cups strawberries

2 bottles vodka – 750 ml each

1 bottle brandy – 750 ml

1 bottle light rum – 750 ml

1 bottle triple sec – 750 ml

2 bottles Kunde Syrah

1 bottle Kunde Cabernet Sauvignon

2 bottles ginger ale – 1.5 L

1 can frozen fruit punch – 12 oz

Preparation:

Cut and freeze the fruit days before and place in quart size freezer baggies. Fill bags less than 1/2 full. Make sure that all of the liquids are pre-chilled ahead of time. Place frozen fruit first in a large glass vessel, add remaining ingredients and stir. Let the party begin!

Serves a crowd.

"I can't make this drink without thinking of Dorothy Parker, an American poet and satirist, (1893-1967) who wrote, 'I can take one martini, two at the very most. Three put me under the table, and four put me under the host!'"

Fresh Garden Tomato Bruschetta

This is a scrumptious recipe from my neighbor Caryn, a wonderful cook. There have been many summer evenings where we've savored these delights over a glass of Chardonnay on our patio. My husband devours these, and he doesn't even like fresh tomatoes!

Ingredients:

1 sourdough baguette – thinly sliced

Olive oil

4 whole large tomatoes – coarsely chopped

2 cloves garlic – crushed

1 bunch fresh basil – chopped

1 tsp kosher salt

Prepared pesto

Parmesan cheese – freshly grated

Preparation:

Preheat oven to 425 degrees. Place sliced sourdough on a foil covered baking sheet and brush the bread with a small amount of olive oil. Bake 8-10 minutes until lightly toasted. Remove from oven and cool.

Combine the chopped tomatoes, garlic, basil, salt and 1 T olive oil in a medium bowl and let stand for 1 hour or more. When ready to serve, brush each crostini with pesto, top with the tomato mixture, and sprinkle with parmesan cheese. Put under broiler briefly to give a quick melt to the cheese. **Serves 6-8**.

Serve with:

Kunde Family Winery Chardonnay – Wildwood Vineyard

"Garden fresh tomatoes really make a big difference in flavor."

Tip:
Buying prepared pesto makes this appetizer a snap.

Ahi Poke Skewers

This recipe is created by Preferred Sonoma Caterers, one of our favorites to work with!

Ingredients:

12 oz sushi-grade ahi tuna

1/2 cup soy sauce

1 lime – juiced

2 T agave syrup

1 T sesame oil

3 green onions – finely sliced

1/2 inch fresh ginger – grated

2 T seasoned rice vinegar

1 T sriracha chili paste – or to taste

1 T toasted sesame seeds – for garnish

Preparation:

Cut the ahi tuna into 3/4 inch cubes. Thread 4-5 pieces on each bamboo skewer. Combine all remaining ingredients, except the sesame seeds, in a small bowl. Place skewers in a shallow baking dish and pour mixture over the top of the skewers. Refrigerate for 15 minutes. Turn skewers and marinate for an additional 15 minutes. When ready to serve, present on a serving tray and sprinkle with the sesame seeds. **Serves 3-4**.

Serve with:

Kunde Family Winery Signature Rosé

Tip:
Don't let the ahi skewers marinate for over 2 hours as you'll lose the wonderful flavor of the fresh ahi.

ESTABLISHED 1904
KUNDE
FAMILY WINERY
Sonoma Valley
MERLOT

Grilled Apricots Stuffed with Blue Cheese, Marcona Almonds and Parma Ham

So yummy, I guarantee you won't be able to eat just one!

Ingredients:

6-8 fresh ripe apricots

Olive oil

Kosher salt

Small wedge of sharp blue cheese

6-8 slices of parma ham – 1/2 slice per apricot

12-16 marcona almonds

Preparation:

Heat grill or grill pan to medium high heat. Halve and pit each apricot. Place apricot halves on a sheet pan and brush with a bit of olive oil and a pinch of salt. Oil grill, then place apricots on grill for 2-3 minutes per side. Let rest for 5 minutes. While apricots are resting, prepare blue cheese and parma ham. Make 12-16 small chunks of blue cheese and set aside in bowl. Slice each piece of parma ham in half.

To assemble, place a chunk of blue cheese in the middle of each apricot half, then add the marcona almond and wrap the ham around each apricot half until secure. Continue to assemble all apricots. You can serve immediately or put under the broiler for 2-3 minutes to crisp up the ham. Watch carefully so it doesn't burn. **Serves 4-6.**

Serve with:

Kunde Family Winery Merlot

"Apricots are the first stone fruit of the summer. This is an easy way to prepare them and oh so good to eat!"

Festive Layered Bean Dip

Always a crowd pleaser and a great appetizer for a sports event.

Ingredients:

Olive oil

1 1/2 cups corn

1 T jalapeño – seeded and finely chopped

1 can black beans – drained

1 bag tortilla chips

1 1/2 cups Monterey Jack cheese – grated

1 cup sour cream

1/4 cup cilantro – chopped, for garnish

Guacamole:

1 large ripe avocado – mashed

1/4 cup red onion – finely diced

1 T fresh lime juice

2 T cilantro – chopped

1 small garlic clove – minced

Salt and pepper

Pico de Gallo:

1 1/2 cups cherry tomatoes – chopped

1 T jalapeño – seeded and finely chopped

1 scallion – finely chopped

1 tsp red wine vinegar

1 T olive oil

2 T cilantro – chopped

Salt and pepper

Preparation:

In a sauté pan over medium heat, drizzle 1-2 T olive oil. Once oil is hot, add corn and jalapeño and sauté for 5 minutes. Add the black beans and sauté for 3-5 more minutes. Turn off heat and set aside.

Combine all guacamole ingredients in a bowl and set aside. Combine all pico de gallo ingredients in another bowl and set aside.

In an oven proof serving dish, layer chips on bottom and sides of the dish and sprinkle with cheese. Broil for 3-5 minutes until cheese is melted. Remove from the oven and let cool for 5 minutes. Add generous dollops of the sour cream, guacamole, and pico de gallo - either on top of each other or in mounds around the dish. Garnish with cilantro and serve immediately. **Serves 4-6**.

Serve with:

Kunde Family Winery Red Dirt Red

Watermelon and Tomato Gazpacho

Super easy—just blend, chill and serve. You'll be craving this refreshing soup on hot summer days.

Ingredients:

1 lb seedless red watermelon

1 large garden fresh red tomato

2 T white balsamic vinegar

1 cup cucumber – peeled

1 jalapeño – seeded and chopped

2 T olive oil

2 T lime juice

Salt to taste

Toppings for serving:

3-5 mint leaves – chiffonade

Cucumber – diced small

Feta cheese – crumbled

Preparation:

Place all ingredients, excluding toppings, in blender and blend until smooth. Taste and adjust lime juice and salt if necessary. Chill for at least one hour before serving. To serve, pour into small shot glasses and sprinkle with mint, cucumber and feta. **Serves 6-8.**

Serve with:

Kunde Family Winery Summer's Blush Rosé

"Summers' finest flavors of sweet watermelon and tangy vine ripened tomatoes make a great appetizer or first course."

Tip:
Place a fresh cut hot pink zinnia on the side for decoration. Gorgeous presentation!

Spinach Strawberry Salad with Marcona Almonds

Serve this pretty summer salad on a white plate and the colors will just pop!

Ingredients:

3 T white balsamic vinegar

1/2 tsp Dijon mustard

1 garlic clove – crushed

1/3 cup olive oil

Salt and pepper

4-5 cups baby spinach leaves

3 cups baby arugula leaves

1 basket fresh strawberries – cleaned and quartered

1/2 cup marcona almonds – chopped

1/2 cup ricotta salata or feta cheese – crumbled

Preparation:

In a medium bowl, whisk together the vinegar, mustard and garlic. Slowly whisk in the olive oil until emulsified. Season with salt and pepper to taste.

In a large salad bowl, gently toss the spinach, arugula, strawberries, marcona almonds, and cheese with the dressing. Serve with freshly ground pepper. **Serves 4-6.**

Serve with:

Kunde Family Winery Chardonnay

Grilled Peach and Arugula Salad with Feta and Spicy Seed Brittle

Light but packed with flavor, this salad makes the perfect dish for a summer garden party.

Ingredients:

3 ripe peaches - halved, pitted and sliced into thirds

Olive oil

Kosher salt

4-5 cups arugula

3/4 cup crumbled feta

Spicy Seed Brittle:

1/2 cup roasted pumpkin seeds

1/4 cup sunflower seeds

1/4 cup sesame seeds

1/2 tsp cayenne pepper

1/4 cup honey

Balsamic Dressing:

1 T balsamic vinegar

1 T lemon juice

Salt and pepper

1 small garlic clove – minced

1 drizzle of honey

1/4 cup olive oil

Preparation:

In a bowl, combine all spicy seed brittle ingredients plus a pinch of salt until well incorporated. Spread on parchment lined sheet pan to 1/8 inch thick with back of spatula. Bake in 350 degree oven until golden brown, about 20 minutes. Once cool, break into small pieces.

While brittle is cooling, prepare the peaches. Brush with olive oil and sprinkle with salt. Heat grill to medium high heat and grill peaches a few minutes per side. Let cool.

To prepare the balsamic dressing, mix balsamic vinegar, lemon juice, salt and pepper, garlic and honey in a bowl. Add 1/4 cup olive oil and whisk until emulsified.

Assemble the salad in a large salad bowl. Toss the arugula with 1-2 T of balsamic dressing. Add peaches, feta and brittle pieces. Toss lightly then serve immediately. **Serves 4**.

Serve with:

Kunde Family Winery Sauvignon Blanc – Block 4SB20

Green Bean Salad with Baby Potatoes and Herb Dijon Vinaigrette

Fresh produce plus a phenomenal vinaigrette makes this a very tasty and versatile salad. Great served alongside lunch, dinner or on its own.

Ingredients:

1 1/2 lbs baby potatoes

2 T olive oil

Salt and pepper

1 lb green beans – trimmed

1 red bell pepper – roasted, peeled, seeded, sliced lengthwise into 1/4 inch strips and then halved

1/2 cup oil cured black olives – pitted and chopped

Herb Dijon Vinaigrette:

2 T champagne vinegar

1 T Dijon mustard

2 tsp honey

2 T shallot – minced

1 garlic clove – minced

2 T Italian parsley – chopped

2 T chives – chopped

4 T olive oil

Salt and pepper

Preparation:

Preheat oven to 400 degrees. Place the potatoes on a sheet pan to roast. Add 2 T oil, a pinch of salt and pepper and toss to combine. Roast in oven for 20-30 minutes until slightly browned and tender. Let cool. Bring a large pot of salted water to boil. Add green beans and cook until just tender, about 5-7 minutes. Transfer beans to an ice bath and then a colander to drain. Transfer beans to a large bowl and add red pepper, olives and potatoes.

To make the vinaigrette, combine the vinegar, mustard, honey, shallot, garlic and herbs in a small bowl and mix well. Slowly whisk in the olive oil until emulsified.

To serve, dress the salad with the vinaigrette and toss to combine. Sprinkle with salt and pepper to taste. Serve at room temperature. Serves 6.

Serve with:

Kunde Family Winery Chardonnay – Wildwood Vineyard

Tip:
Pick the beans fresh from the garden before they get too large and stringy. Small to mid-size beans are the best.

Fresh Corn Chowder with Crispy Bacon

Fresh sweet corn and bacon make for a rich and flavorful summertime soup.

Ingredients:

Olive oil

7 slices pancetta or bacon – cut into small pieces

3 cloves garlic – minced

1 yellow onion – chopped

1 celery stalk – diced

1 small leek – cleaned and chopped

1/3 cup Chardonnay

1 poblano chili pepper

2 yukon gold potatoes – small dice

3 fresh thyme sprigs

4-5 cups chicken stock

5 ears fresh corn – kernels cut off the cob, approximately 4 cups

1/2 cup heavy cream

2 T lemon juice

Salt and pepper

Cilantro – chopped, for garnish

Preparation:

In a large heavy pot, heat 1 T olive oil over medium heat. Add bacon and sauté until crispy, 5-7 minutes. Remove 1/2 of the bacon and set aside in bowl for garnish. Add garlic, onion, celery and leek to remaining bacon and cook for 5-7 minutes until onion and leek are soft. Add 1/3 cup Chardonnay and cook over medium heat until reduced by half.

Meanwhile, prepare the poblano chili pepper. Char over a flame and then sweat in a closed zip lock bag for 10 minutes. Remove stem, seeds, skin and chop finely. Set aside.

Add potatoes, thyme, and stock to the large pot and simmer until potatoes are soft, about 10 minutes. Add corn and chopped poblano chili pepper. Season to taste with salt and pepper. Simmer to cook corn through about 10 more minutes. Discard the thyme sprigs. Add cream and lemon juice. Stir well. Take immersion blender and blend pulsing 4-5 times or until desired consistency. Serve immediately with bacon bits and cilantro as garnish. **Serves 6.**

Serve with:

Kunde Family Winery Chardonnay – Wildwood Vineyard

Tip:
You can use frozen corn to create this summer soup but nothing is better than fresh corn kernels cut off the cob.

Sriracha Lime Grilled Fish Tacos

Quick, fresh and addicting. Citrus marinated fish topped with a sriracha ranch dressing. A true delight!

Ingredients:

1 1/2 lbs of halibut fillets

3 T olive oil

2 limes – juiced

Salt and pepper

3/4 cup ranch salad dressing

2 T sriracha sauce – more if you like it spicy

12 small corn tortillas

2 cups of shredded red cabbage

1/2 cup green onion – chopped

1 cup prepared guacamole

Cilantro – chopped, for garnish

1 lime – cut into wedges

Tip:
I use fresh halibut for my fish tacos but you can use any firm, mild flavored fish.

Preparation:

Marinate the fish in the olive oil, lime juice, salt and pepper for 30 minutes. Prepare the dressing by combining the ranch dressing and sriracha sauce in a small bowl. Set aside. Preheat oven to 250 degrees, wrap tortillas in foil and bake for 5 to 10 minutes or until warm.

Preheat the barbecue to medium heat. Remove fish from marinade and place on the grill. Grill fish until cooked through, but not overdone. Build the taco with fish, cabbage, onion, guacamole and top with the sriracha ranch dressing, cilantro and a squeeze of fresh lime juice. **Serves 3-4.**

Serve with:

Kunde Family Winery Sauvignon Blanc - Block 4SB20 or a fresh margarita!

"You can heat tortillas on grill (as pictured) or bake in an oven - whichever you prefer."

4th, 5th, 6th generation Kundes

Looking for lizards

Zin, peaches and mint

Halibut with Fennel, Olives and Cherry Tomatoes

A beautiful mélange of flavors to enjoy with my favorite fish.

Ingredients:

1 fennel bulb – thinly sliced (reserve fennel fronds for garnish)

1 small onion – thinly sliced

Olive oil

2 garlic cloves – sliced

1 lemon – thinly sliced

Salt and pepper

4 halibut fillets, 4-5 oz each – skinned and deboned

1 cup kalamata olives – pits removed

1 cup cherry tomatoes – halved

1/2 cup Chardonnay

3 T butter – cut into small chunks

Preparation:

In large skillet over medium heat, sauté fennel and onion in 2 T olive oil for 5 minutes. Add garlic, lemon, salt and pepper and sauté for 2-3 minutes more. Transfer to a plate and set aside. In same skillet over medium-high heat, add more olive oil and cook halibut on each side for 3-5 minutes. Add fennel mixture back into skillet, arranging around the fish. Then add olives, tomatoes and wine.

Cover and cook for 3-4 minutes. Remove lid and add butter. Cook for a few more minutes. Add salt and pepper to taste if needed. Plate the fish and serve drizzled with pan juices and fresh fennel fronds. **Serves 3-4.**

Serve with:

Kunde Family Winery Reserve Chardonnay

Grilled Chicken with Corn and Green Chili Salsa

So easy to prepare...grab a few friends, a few bottles of Chardonnay, and you've got a fiesta!

Ingredients:

4-6 chicken thighs

Olive oil

Salt and pepper

Lime wedges for garnish

Corn and Chili Salsa:

2 poblano chili peppers – charred, skinned and chopped

3 corn cobs – charred and cut kernels from cob

2 scallions – chopped

1 cup cilantro – chopped

2 T lime juice

1/4 cup olive oil

Preparation:

Prepare the corn and chili salsa first. Preheat barbecue or grill pan on medium high heat. Cook the corn and chilies until charred, about 5 minutes. Put the chilies in a zip lock bag and sweat for 10 minutes. Cut the corn kernels from the cob and place in bowl. Remove skin from the chilies, discard seeds and chop. Add to the corn. Add scallions, cilantro, lime juice and a few drizzles of olive oil. Check seasoning and add salt, pepper and more lime juice if needed.

Brush chicken thighs with olive oil and sprinkle with salt and pepper. Grill chicken until cooked through, about 8-10 minutes. Serve chicken whole or sliced with the corn and chili salsa and lime wedges. **Serves 3-4.**

Serve with:

Kunde Family Winery Reserve Chardonnay

"Great summertime fare, especially with fresh picked corn from the garden."

Citrus Bok Choy, Shiitake Mushrooms and Beef Stir-Fry over Rice

Fresh veggies and tender beef make this stir-fry a standout at the dinner table.

Ingredients:

Olive oil

1 1/2 lbs New York steak - sliced 1/4 inch thick

3-4 tangerines – zest and set aside. Juice tangerines and set aside for the Citrus Sauce

6 oz shiitake mushrooms – sliced

4-5 baby bok choy – cut into quarter wedges

1 small fennel bulb – sliced thinly

3 garlic cloves – chopped

1 T ginger – finely chopped

4 scallions – slice thinly, separate white parts and use green as garnish

Rice or thin Asian noodles

Citrus Sauce:

1/2 cup tangerine juice

2 T hoisin sauce

1/4 cup soy sauce

1 tsp honey

2 T seasoned rice vinegar

2 T toasted sesame oil

1 1/2 tsp cornstarch

1 tsp garlic chili sauce

Garnish:

Sesame seeds

Scallion greens

Preparation:

Combine ingredients for citrus sauce and set aside. Heat a large, heavy sauté pan or wok over medium-high heat until hot. Add 1 T oil. Add beef in a single layer, cook 1-2 minutes until nicely brown on each side. Repeat with remaining beef. Reserve beef on a large platter, cover with foil and keep warm. Add 1 T oil to the pan and sauté mushrooms 3-4 minutes. Add to the beef platter. Add a bit more oil and the bok choy. Sauté 3-5 minutes and arrange on platter. Sauté fennel 2-3 minutes and add to platter. Add 1 T oil, garlic, ginger and white scallion slices and sauté 1-2 minutes. Add the citrus zest and the citrus sauce, cook for an additional 2-3 minutes until bubbling and hot. Drizzle sauce over platter and garnish with sesame seeds and scallion greens. Serve immediately with rice or thin Asian noodles. **Serves 3-4**.

Serve with:
Kunde Family Winery Red Dirt Red

Tip:
Have all your ingredients prepared and at the ready when you start cooking this dish.

Summer Beef and Plum Pizzettes

A great recipe for summer when plums are at their peak of flavor.

Ingredients:

1 large rib eye steak

2 naan flat breads

Olive oil

2 red plums – thinly sliced

1 to 2 T honey

Small red onion – thinly sliced

1/2 cup blue cheese – crumbled

3 T salted pistachio nuts – chopped

Fresh thyme – chopped

Salt and pepper

Tip:

For a toastier crust, place the naan directly on the oven rack, or even better, over the barbecue grill. If grilling, keep the flame very low and close the barbecue lid.

Preparation:

Preheat your barbecue. Grill steaks until rare or your preference of desired doneness. Be aware steak is cooked again in oven below. Remove from the grill and slice thinly across the grain. Set aside.

Preheat oven to 425 degrees. Place flat breads on a baking sheet. Brush the bread with a fine layering of olive oil. Top with 6 to 7 slices of plum. Drizzle honey over the top. Divide beef slices between the two pieces of naan. Arrange thin slices of red onion followed by blue cheese crumbles, chopped pistachios, and fresh thyme. Salt and pepper to taste. Place in the oven for approximately 10 -12 minutes, until the blue cheese begins to melt. **Serves 3-4.**

Serve with:

Kunde Family Winery Syrah

Roasted Red Pepper and Hamburger Pizza with Smoked Mozzarella and Fresh Arugula

A different take on fresh home cooked pizza.

Ingredients:

1 yellow onion – cut in half, thinly sliced

Olive oil

Salt and pepper

1 tsp fresh thyme

1/2 lb ground beef

2-3 garlic cloves – minced

1/2 cup roasted red pepper – thinly sliced

1 pizza dough – homemade or any store-bought crust,
rolled out 12-14 inches.

1 1/2 cups smoked mozzarella – shredded

1-2 cups fresh arugula

Preparation:

Preheat grill on high heat or oven to 500 degrees. Pre-heat pizza stone for 30 minutes before cooking pizza.

Cook onion in 1-2 T of olive oil over medium low heat for 20 minutes or until caramelized. Add salt, pepper, fresh thyme and set aside. In a separate pan, cook ground beef in 1 T olive oil over medium heat for 3 minutes with 1 crushed garlic clove and salt and pepper to taste. Continue cooking until browned. Drain off grease and set aside in bowl. Char pepper over open flame and place in plastic bag for 5 minutes to loosen skin, then peel and slice thinly.

Flour or corn meal the pan or pizza stone to ensure crust doesn't stick. Brush 1 T of olive oil and one crushed garlic clove over crust. Add shredded cheese evenly, ground beef, onions and peppers. Bake on hot pizza stone until cheese is melted and sides are crispy brown, about 4-8 minutes. Serve pizza garnished with fresh arugula and a drizzle of olive oil. **Serves 3-4**.

Serve with:
Kunde Family Winery Merlot

Caprese Burger

These scrumptious burgers make a quick weeknight meal or great party time sliders.

Ingredients:

1 1/4 lbs ground beef

2 garlic cloves – minced

Salt and pepper

5 oz ball fresh mozzarella – sliced into 1/4 inch thick slices, dried with a towel

1 French baguette – sliced into 4 inch pieces, sliced in half, brushed with olive oil

1 large tomato – sliced into rounds

5-7 large basil leaves

Pesto Sauce:

1 1/2 cups basil

1/3 cup pine nuts

1/2 cup olive oil

1 garlic clove

Squeeze of lemon juice

Salt and pepper

Preparation:

Place all ingredients for the pesto sauce into blender and blend until smooth. Taste, add salt, pepper and lemon juice as needed.

Mix beef with garlic, salt and pepper. Divide beef into 4 even-sized balls and shape each ball into a 1/2 inch thick rectangle. Grill burgers to desired doneness, then add fresh mozzarella slice on top of burger and melt slightly. Remove and cover with foil to keep warm. Toast bread slices on grill.

To assemble the burgers, spread pesto on baguette, top with burger, place a basil leaf or two on mozzarella, then tomato. Serve immediately. **Serves 4.**

Serve with:
Kunde Family Winery Cabernet Sauvignon

"Mozzarella is great melted on the patty or cold. Any style of bread works, so use your favorite!"

Tip:
With your pesto sauce, fresh is best but if you're in a jam for time, pre-made pesto is a great time saver.

Skirt Steak with Red Chimichurri

You'll love this red chimichurri sauce—easy to make and packed with flavor!

Ingredients:

1 1/2 lbs skirt steak

Salt and pepper

2 garlic cloves – crushed

1 cup greek yogurt

1 package flatbread or naan

Olive oil

Fresh cilantro sprigs for garnish

Red Chimichurri Sauce:

1/4 cup roasted piquillo peppers or red peppers

1 cup cherry tomatoes

1/4 cup red onion

1 garlic clove

3 T parsley

3 T cilantro

1/2 tsp chili flakes

1/2 tsp smoked paprika

1/2 tsp ground cumin

1/4 cup extra virgin olive oil

1 T red wine vinegar

1 T lemon juice

Salt and pepper

Preparation:

Place all sauce ingredients in a food processor and process just until incorporated and slightly chunky. Salt and pepper to taste.

Place steak on a sheet pan, salt and pepper, spread crushed garlic and drizzle with olive oil. Let steak rest for 30 minutes to 1 hour before grilling. Preheat grill or grill pan on high heat. It's very important to have a hot grill because the skirt steak needs a good sear, 4-7 minutes per side. Let the steak rest 6-8 minute before slicing. Slice the meat against the grain into 1/4 inch strips. While meat is resting grill flatbread over medium heat.

Place the skirt steak strips over flatbreads with a dollop of greek yogurt, chimichurri sauce and fresh cilantro. **Serves 4**.

Serve with:
Kunde Family Winery Meritage 202

Tip:

If you prefer a more traditional green Chimichurri sauce, try this one with bacon.

4 garlic cloves

1/2 cup flat leaf parsley

1/4 cup oregano leaves

1/4 cup seasoned rice vinegar

1 lemon – juiced

1 cup olive oil

Salt and pepper

1/2 lb sliced bacon

Combine all ingredients except bacon until puréed. Cook bacon until crisp, remove from pan, drain, cool and chop. Pour all fat from pan except 2T. When meat is resting, heat bacon fat in pan, pour chimichurri sauce into pan and bring to a simmer over high heat. Remove from heat, and stir in chopped bacon.

Grilled Rib Eye Steaks with Caramelized Onions and Blue Cheese

Who doesn't love a juicy steak? My choice of beef—Sonoma Mountain Beef Co. of course!

Ingredients:

4 rib eye steaks

Olive oil

Salt and pepper

2 T butter

2 sweet yellow onions – halved and sliced into 1/4" slices

1 T fresh thyme

1 tsp honey

2 tsp balsamic vinegar

1 blue cheese wedge – room temperature

Preparation:

Brush steaks with olive oil, sprinkle with salt and pepper and set aside 1 hour before grilling. Allow 30+ minutes to caramelize onions. Using a medium high heat, melt butter, 2 T olive oil and sliced onions, thyme, a pinch of salt and stir occasionally. After about 30 minutes, add honey and balsamic vinegar and cook for about 5 more minutes. Spoon onions into a bowl and set aside. Slice blue cheese and set aside.

Heat grill to medium high and brush grates with oil. Grill steaks for 5-10 minutes per side. Internal temperature for medium rare is 125 degrees. Let steaks rest for 5-8 minutes.

Place rib eye steaks on a platter or individual plates, spoon over caramelized onions and top with a slice of blue cheese. Serve immediately. **Serves 4.**

Serve with:

Kunde Family Winery Cabernet Sauvignon – Drummond

Marinated Strawberries Divine

Incredibly simple to make and outrageously elegant and delicious.

Ingredients:

1/2 bottle Syrah

1/2 cup sugar

3 baskets fresh strawberries – sliced

Vanilla ice cream

Sprigs of fresh mint leaves

Preparation:

Mix wine and sugar together until sugar is dissolved. Stir in sliced strawberries. Let marinate for a minimum of 3 hours but if time allows, overnight is best.

Place a large scoop of vanilla ice cream in the bottom of a large bowl or glass. Spoon the strawberry/wine mixture over the top and garnish with a sprig of fresh mint. **Serves 4.**

Serve with:

Kunde Family Winery 1904 Dessert Cuvée

"I love serving this dessert in a beautiful red wine glass for a simple, yet elegant, presentation!"

Tip:
Make this early in the day in order to let the strawberries completely marinate and meld with the flavors of the wine.

Rustic Cherry Apricot Tart

Seasonal fruit and a flaky crust combine to make this a fantastic finale at dinner.

Ingredients:

3 cups cherries – pitted and halved

1-2 T sugar

1-2 T lemon juice – freshly squeezed

5-7 ripe apricots – seeded and sliced into 1/4 inch sections

1 lb ricotta cheese

1 T lemon zest

1/2 cup almond slices – toasted

Drizzle of honey

Tart Dough:

1 1/3 cups flour

1/3 cup almond flour

1 tsp sugar

Pinch of salt

11 T cold butter – cut into small cubes

1/3 cup ice water

2 T heavy cream

Preparation:

Prepare the tart dough first. Put the two flours, sugar and salt in food processor and pulse to combine. Add cold butter and pulse several times until mixture is slightly coarse with small chunks of butter. Add ice water slowly and pulse a few more times to incorporate. Check to see if dough holds together by squeezing. Place dough in plastic wrap and press into a circle. Chill for 1 hour. Heat oven to 350 degrees. Roll out dough into a rectangle on parchment about 1/4 inch thick. Transfer to a sheet pan. Chill for 15 minutes in freezer or refrigerator then brush with cream, or if you prefer an egg wash, and bake for 20-30 minutes until golden brown. Transfer to rack and let cool completely.

Toss cherries with 1-2 T of sugar (depending on how sweet the cherries are), 1 T lemon juice and a pinch of salt. Let sit at room temperature for 30 minutes or more. In a separate bowl, toss apricots with a little sugar depending on sweetness, 1 tsp lemon juice and a pinch of salt. Mix ricotta cheese with 1 T lemon zest.

To assemble, spread ricotta on cooled crust, top with cherries and apricots, sprinkle with toasted almonds and drizzle with honey. Cut into squares and serve. **Serves 8-10**.

Serve with:

Kunde Family Winery 1904 Dessert Cuvée

Plum Berry Crumble

Top your seasonal fruit with this yummy coconut crust and a dollop of ice cream for a perfectly sweet treat!

Ingredients:

6 - 8 ripe plums – pitted and sliced into 1/2 inch wedges

1 cup ripe berries – raspberry, boysenberry or blueberry

1 T sugar

1 T lemon juice

2 T flour

Pinch of salt

Crumble Topping:

1 1/4 cups flour

1/2 cup unsweetened shredded coconut

1/2 cup butter – cold and cut into small cubes

1/3 cup almonds – toasted and sliced

2 T candied ginger – chopped (optional)

Tip:
You can use any combination of berries for this dessert or, just one.

Preparation:

To prepare the fruit, mix the plums, berries, sugar, lemon juice, flour, salt and let sit while preparing the crumble topping. For crumble topping, mix the flour, coconut and butter together, rubbing in the butter with your fingertips until well incorporated. Add almonds and ginger.

Spoon the fruit mixture into a greased pie dish and spoon crumble mixture on top. Bake at 350 degrees for 20-30 minutes until topping starts to brown. Let cool and serve with vanilla ice cream or a dollop of greek yogurt. **Serves 4-6.**

Serve with:

Kunde Family Winery Sweet Leslie

Red Velvet Cake with Summer Berries

My friend Sheila shared this colorful recipe and I make it every year for the Fourth of July.

Ingredients:

2-3 small to medium red beets

2 1/4 cups sifted cake flour

2 T unsweetened Dutch process cocoa powder

2 tsp baking powder

1/2 tsp salt

1 cup buttermilk – room temperature

2 T lemon juice

2 tsp white vinegar

1 tsp vanilla

1 1/2 cups sugar

1/2 cup unsalted butter – softened

2 eggs

Cream Cheese Frosting:

2, 8 oz packages cream cheese – softened

1/2 cup unsalted butter – softened

1 T vanilla

2 1/2 cups powdered sugar

3 small baskets each of fresh raspberries and blueberries – rinsed and dried

Tip: To achieve a true red color, skip beets, add 1 T of red food coloring and replace 1 tsp of baking powder with 1 tsp of baking soda.

Preparation:

Preheat oven to 350 degrees. Wash beets, wrap in aluminum foil and bake until tip of knife easily pierces the beet, about 1 1/2 hours. Cool beets, peel and process in a food processor until finely chopped. Measure 1 cup of the puree and set aside.

Preheat oven to 350 degrees. Butter and flour two 9 inch round cake pans. In a medium bowl, combine the flour, cocoa powder, baking powder, salt and mix well. Pour cup of beet puree back in the food processor, add buttermilk, lemon juice, vinegar, vanilla and puree until smooth. In a large bowl, use an electric mixer and beat sugar and butter until well blended. Add eggs 1 at a time, beating well. Mix in dry ingredients in 3 equal amounts alternating with 2 additions of the buttermilk/beet mixture. Pour the batter evenly between the two prepared cake pans. Bake for approximately 25 minutes or until a toothpick comes out clean. Cool cake completely before frosting.

For frosting, beat cream cheese and butter in a large bowl until fully blended. Add vanilla, powdered sugar and mix until smooth and fully blended. Place 1 cake layer on a cake plate and spread 1 cup frosting over top. Place berries on top of frosting, pressing lightly to adhere. Place second cake layer on top and finish with the remaining frosting over top and sides of cake. Arrange remaining berries decoratively over top of cake and along bottom. Serves 8-10.

Serve with:

Kunde Family Winery 1904 Dessert Cuvée

Winery groundbreaking-1990

Dog days of Summmer

Our supreme champion Frisky with Jamie

Winemaker Zach

Cute lil' pumpkin!

Fall

The sweet scent of mouthwatering fresh crushed grape juice fills the air as the vineyards come alive at harvest. Crisp mornings turn to heated afternoons, ripening and preparing the grapes for their journey to the crush pad. Vineyards are ablaze with color as the tender green leaves turn to the vibrant yellow and red hues of autumn harvest. Electric with activity, the winery hums as the production crews scurry about to fill the tanks and barrels with the bounty of nature's beauty.

Harvest Pear and Caramelized Onion Crostini

This tasty appetizer is so reflective of autumn—pears, caramelized onions and blue cheese. Yum!

Ingredients:

1 sourdough baguette – thinly sliced

Olive oil

3 T butter

3 sweet yellow onions – thinly sliced

4 Anjou or Bartlett pears – washed, peeled, cut in half, cored and cut into thin slices

2 T balsamic vinegar

2 T honey or maple syrup

Salt and pepper

1 1/2 cups crumbled blue cheese

3/4 cup walnuts – toasted and coarsely chopped

Preparation:

Preheat oven to 425 degrees. Place sliced sourdough on a foil covered baking sheet and brush the bread with a small amount of olive oil. Bake 8-10 minutes until lightly toasted. Remove from oven and cool.

In a large sauté pan, add 2 T olive oil and 2 T of the butter and cook on low heat until butter is melted. Add sliced yellow onions and continue to cook on low heat until caramelized, about 25 minutes. Place onions in separate bowl to cool. Add the remaining 1 T of butter to the pan and sauté pears for about 5 minutes or until tender. Combine the balsamic vinegar, honey or maple syrup with the onions and add salt and pepper to taste.

Place a small amount of blue cheese on top of each crostini, followed by a spoonful of the onion mixture, then pear slices and finally the chopped walnuts. Return the crostini to the oven and bake for about 4 minutes. Remove and serve warm. **Serves 8-10**.

Serve with:

Kunde Family Winery Reserve Chardonnay

Beef Crostini with Orange Zest and Toasted Pumpkin Seeds

A delectable treat created by our talented friends at Park Avenue Catering.

Ingredients:

1 sourdough baguette – thinly sliced

Olive oil

1 Valencia orange – zested

1 lb beef tenderloin – trimmed

1 oz blackened spice

1/2 cup pumpkin seeds – toasted

Cabernet Reduction:

2 T shallots – chopped

1 T butter

1 bay leaf

10 black peppercorns

2 sprigs Italian parsley

3/4 cup Cabernet Sauvignon

1 cup beef broth

Salt and pepper

Preparation:

Preheat oven to 425 degrees. Place sliced sourdough on a foil covered baking sheet and brush the bread with a small amount of olive oil. Bake 8-10 minutes until lightly toasted. Remove from oven and cool.

Finely zest the Valencia orange and dry in the oven at 350 degrees for 2-3 minutes. Set aside. Rub the tenderloin with blackened spice. Sear first and then roast in a 350 degree oven for approximately 7-10 minutes or until meat thermometer reaches 120 degrees. Remove from oven, cover and let rest.

To prepare the Cabernet reduction sauce, sweat the shallots with butter until golden. Add bay leaf, peppercorns, parsley, Cabernet Sauvignon and reduce 60%. Add beef broth and cook until reduced by half. Season sauce with salt and pepper to taste.

To serve, slice tenderloin thinly, approximately same size as crostini. Top each crostini with a piece of tenderloin, a drizzle of Cabernet reduction sauce, dried orange zest and toasted pumpkin seeds. **Serves 8-10.**

Serve with:
Kunde Family Winery Malbec

Roasted Fig Salad with Fresh Ricotta, Honey Walnuts and Pomegranate Seeds

If you love figs, this salad will put a smile on your face.

Ingredients:

8-10 fresh figs – trimmed and halved

1 T balsamic vinegar

2 T olive oil

2 T honey – divided

1/2 cup walnuts – chopped

4 large handfuls of mixed salad greens

1/2 cup fresh ricotta

1/4 cup pomegranate seeds

Vinaigrette:

2 T lemon juice

2 T orange juice

1 tsp honey

5 T olive oil

Salt and pepper

Preparation:

Prepare figs and place on baking sheet. Mix balsamic vinegar, olive oil and 1 T honey in a small dish, then drizzle over each fig. Roast in 400 degree oven for 5-8 minutes, until they begin to caramelize a bit. Remove from oven and let cool.

Toss together walnuts, 1 T honey and toast in oven for 5-8 minutes. Remove from oven and let cool. Note: Walnuts and figs can share the same oven. While figs and walnuts are roasting, make the vinaigrette by whisking all the dressing ingredients together. If necessary, adjust citrus, salt and pepper to desired taste.

To prepare salad, place mixed greens in a bowl and toss with some of the vinaigrette. Next arrange the figs and ricotta chunks around bowl and sprinkle walnuts and pomegranate seeds on top. Drizzle reserved vinaigrette to taste. **Serves 4.**

Serve with:

Kunde Family Winery Chardonnay – Wildwood Vineyard

Tip:
You can also serve this on individual plates for a lovely presentation.

Roasted Pear and Blue Cheese Harvest Salad with Balsamic Vinaigrette

Tangy blue cheese accentuates the sweet flavors of fresh pears and dried cranberries.

Ingredients:

2/3 cup blue cheese – crumbled

Pepper

3 Bartlett pears – ripe but firm

Juice of 1 lemon

6 large handfuls of mixed salad greens

1/2 cup dried cranberries

Balsamic Vinaigrette:

1 T balsamic vinegar

1 T freshly squeezed lemon juice

1 T Dijon mustard

1 garlic clove – chopped

1 tsp honey

1/3 cup olive oil

Salt and pepper

Preparation:

To prepare the vinaigrette, whisk all dressing ingredients together except the olive oil. Slowly whisk in olive oil until emulsified. Taste and adjust salt and pepper as needed.

Preheat the oven to 400 degrees. In a small bowl, mix together the blue cheese and pepper and set aside. Cut pears in 1/2 lengthwise and toss gently in the lemon juice. Place pears in a greased baking dish with the cut sides up and bake for 10 minutes.

Take pears out of the oven, add blue cheese to each pear cavity and then bake 5-8 minutes more until the cheese is bubbling.

To prepare the salad, place a generous portion of salad greens on 6 salad plates. Slice each pear half as you would a fan and place over the salad greens. Drizzle with vinaigrette and sprinkle with dried cranberries. **Serves 6.**

Serve with:

Kunde Family Winery Chardonnay – Wildwood Vineyard

Caramelized Apple Salad with Blue Cheese, Walnuts and Dijon Dressing

I'm a big fan of blue cheese and this combination of caramelized apples and walnuts provides wonderful layers of flavors.

Ingredients:

2 T butter

2 apples – halved, cored and sliced into 1/4 inch wedges

1 T honey

4-6 large handfuls of mixed salad greens

3/4 cup blue cheese – crumbled

1/2 cup walnuts – toasted and chopped

Dijon Dressing:

1 T apple cider vinegar

1/4 cup olive oil

1 tsp Dijon mustard

1 tsp honey

Salt and pepper

Preparation:

Prepare the dressing by whisking all ingredients together in a medium bowl and set aside.

To prepare the apples, melt butter in large sauté pan over medium heat, add apples and cook for 5 minutes, turning occasionally. Drizzle honey over the apples and continue to cook and stir until slightly brown and caramelized. Place apples on a plate to cool.

To prepare the salad, toss greens with the dressing (may not require all dressing) then add apples, blue cheese, walnuts and serve immediately. **Serves 4-6.**

Serve with:

Kunde Family Winery Chardonnay – C.S. Ridge Vineyard

"By the time fall arrives, the selection of fresh apples is tremendous. Honey Crisp and Pink Lady are two of my favorites."

Heirloom Tomato Soup with Parmesan Crostini

Easy to prepare and full of the flavors of fall—the perfect warm treat on a cool autumn day.

Ingredients:

4 lbs heirloom tomatoes – halved

4 cloves garlic – skinned and halved

Salt and pepper

2 tsp maple syrup

1/4 cup olive oil

1 cup basil leaves – stems removed

1 tsp champagne vinegar

Parmesan crostini or croutons for garnish

Prepared pesto sauce for garnish

Preparation:

Place halved tomatoes on sheet pan with garlic. Sprinkle with 1 tsp salt, maple syrup, and olive oil. Gently mix and then roast in a 375 degree oven for 30 minutes. Remove from oven and let cool. Gently remove the skins from the tomatoes.

Transfer tomatoes and garlic to a large soup pot adding basil and vinegar. Using an immersion blender, blend until smooth. If you don't have an immersion blender, strain the soup through a sieve to create the smooth texture. Over medium heat, bring the soup to a hot temperature to serve. Salt and pepper to taste. Serve with parmesan crostini or croutons, a drizzle of olive oil or an herb pesto, if desired. **Serves 6-8.**

Serve with:
Kunde Family Winery Chardonnay

"Who doesn't love a savory roasted tomato soup created from zesty, sweet garden tomatoes?"

Curried Butternut Squash Soup

A beautiful color and delicious flavor. Who knew squash could taste so good!

Ingredients:

1 whole butternut squash

1 yellow onion – diced

Salt and pepper

2 T olive oil

2 apples – peeled and diced

2 tsp curry powder

4-5 cups chicken or vegetable stock

2 tsp maple syrup

2 tsp lemon juice

Crème fraîche and chives for garnish

Preparation:

Peel the squash, scoop out the seeds, and chop into 2" pieces. Sauté onion in stock pot over medium heat with a pinch of salt and olive oil for 5 minutes. Add apples, curry and cook for a few more minutes. Next, add the squash and just enough stock to cover the onions, apples and squash. Simmer for approximately 30 minutes or until the apples and squash are completely cooked through.

Remove from heat and purée mixture in a blender in 2-3 batches until smooth or if preferred, use an immersion blender in the stock pot. Return mixture to the stove, add maple syrup, lemon juice, and salt and pepper to taste. Taste and adjust seasoning if necessary. Soup may need to be thinned with a bit more stock. Cook on low heat for 5-8 more minutes. Serve in soup bowls and garnish with a dollop of crème fraîche and chives. **Serves 4-6.**

Serve with:

Kunde Family Winery Chardonnay

Tip:

Roasting the squash, onion and apples will add extra richness to this soup. Using parchment lined sheet pans and a 400 degree oven, roast squash with olive oil, 1 tsp of curry powder, salt and pepper for about 20-25 minutes until slightly caramelized and golden brown on the edges. For apples and onions, cut in similar sized pieces, add same spices and roast for about 15 minutes. Then place all roasted ingredients in a soup pot, add stock and cook for 10 minutes. Blend for a smooth consistency, return mixture to stove and add maple syrup, lemon juice, salt and pepper to taste. Add more stock for desired consistency.

Miso-Glazed Salmon with Shiitake Mushroom Rice

The savory miso glaze highlights the wonderful richness of fresh salmon.

Ingredients:

4-5 oz salmon fillets – pin bones removed

1/4 cup white miso paste

2 T seasoned rice vinegar

1 T honey

1 T soy sauce

1 T toasted sesame oil

1/4 cup scallions for garnish – thinly sliced

Shiitake Mushroom Rice:

7 dried shiitake mushrooms

7 fresh shiitake mushrooms – thinly sliced

2 cloves garlic – chopped

2-3 T olive oil

2 cups white rice – rinsed

Salt and pepper

Preparation:

Place salmon fillets on parchment lined baking sheet. Prepare the marinade by mixing together the miso, vinegar, honey, soy sauce and sesame oil in a small bowl. Generously spread the marinade over each salmon fillet. Let marinate for 1 hour minimum or up to 3 hours in the refrigerator.

While the fish is marinating, prepare and cook the rice. Place dried shiitake mushrooms in 3 1/2 cups boiling water, turn off heat and let sit for 10-15 minutes. Use this water to cook rice. While dried mushrooms are steeping, sauté fresh mushrooms and garlic in olive oil over medium high heat for 5-8 minutes until soft. Set aside. Remove dried shiitake mushrooms from liquid and slice. Put rice in medium sauce pan and add shiitake water and sliced dried mushrooms. Cover, bring to a simmer, then lower heat and cook for 30-40 minutes or until rice is tender. Fluff rice with fork, add sautéed mushrooms, garlic and salt and pepper to taste. Drizzle a bit more olive oil if needed.

To cook the salmon, pre-heat the broiler and cook for about 5 minutes. Check for doneness and then continue to cook for about 3 more minutes, being careful not to overcook. You want to have a nice caramelization of the miso glaze. Serve immediately with shiitake mushroom rice and garnish with scallions. **Serves 4-6.**

Serve with:

Kunde Family Winery Chardonnay – Wildwood Vineyard

Mushroom Risotto with Prawns and Saffron

I was originally inspired to make risotto by family friend Sylvia Sebastiani. I've adapted her recipe over the years and added prawns and a wonderful cheese, crafted by my friend Karen from her Jersey cows raised on the northern California coast.

Ingredients:

1 cup butter – divided

1/2 lb fresh white mushrooms – sliced

1 yellow onion – diced

1 1/2 cups arborio rice

1/8 tsp powdered saffron

1 cup + 2 T Chardonnay

4-5 cups low sodium chicken broth

1 lb large prawns – peeled and deveined

3 T butter

2 cloves garlic – minced

Pinch of red pepper flakes

Salt and pepper

1/2 cup Estero Gold cheese (or other firm nutty style cheese) – grated

1/2 cup parmesan cheese – grated

Tip:
If you're not a fan of prawns, it's just as tasty without them.

Preparation:

Melt 3 T butter in a sauté pan over medium-low heat. Add sliced mushrooms and sauté until the mushrooms are soft and lightly browned. Remove from heat and set aside. Melt 1/2 cup butter in a large heavy stock pot, add onions and sauté very slowly, stirring frequently until soft, about 10-15 minutes, without browning. Add rice, mushrooms and stir gently for a minute or two, combining well with the butter. Dissolve saffron in 2 T of heated Chardonnay, then add to the rice along with 3/4 cup Chardonnay. Add chicken broth a little bit at a time, stirring for about 30 minutes until the rice is tender and all of the liquid is absorbed.

While the risotto is cooking, prepare the prawns. Melt 2 T of butter over medium-low heat with the garlic. Stir in 1/4 cup Chardonnay followed by prawns and sauté until prawns are no longer pink and are cooked through. Add a pinch of red pepper flakes and salt and pepper to taste. Set aside and keep warm.

For final prep of the risotto, stir in the two cheeses just before serving. Add salt and pepper to taste.

To serve, place a large spoonful of the risotto on to a plate or shallow soup bowl followed by 3-4 prawns fanned out on top of the risotto. If you like, you can sprinkle a little freshly grated parmesan over the top. **Serves 6.**

Serve with:

Kunde Family Winery Reserve Chardonnay

fresh harvest
Juice

KUNDE
ESTABLISHED 1904
FAMILY WINERY

Cooper and Marley
ready to go!

Pasta Vino

A delicious and hearty tomato based pasta dish that's great for a crowd or just a few.

Ingredients:

1 large yellow onion – chopped

3 T olive oil

5 sweet Italian sausages – skinned and crumbled

3/4 lb mushrooms – sliced

3 T fresh basil – chopped

1/4 cup red wine

2 cups canned Italian plum tomatoes – chopped

4 T whole milk or half and half

Salt and pepper

1 lb rigatoni pasta

1 cup Pecorino Romano cheese – shaved

Fresh basil leaves for garnish

Preparation:

In a saucepan over medium heat, sauté the onion in the olive oil until translucent and tender. Add sausages and cook for 5 minutes or until slightly browned, ensuring the sausage is broken into bite sized pieces. Add the mushrooms, basil and red wine. Cook until the wine reduces a bit, about 3 minutes. Add the tomatoes, let simmer for 8 minutes and then add milk, salt and pepper to taste. Remove from heat.

Bring a large pot of salted water to a boil and cook the rigatoni according to package directions. Drain and return the pasta to the pot. Add the sausage/tomato sauce and mix well with the pasta.

To serve, place pasta in individual heated serving bowls and sprinkle with cheese. Garnish with a basil leaf for a nice decorative touch. **Serves 4-6.**

Serve with:
Kunde Family Winery Red Dirt Red

Tip:
Serve this flavor-filled pasta dish with a green salad dressed in a vinaigrette and a fresh loaf of sourdough. Delizioso!

Caramelized Onion and Mushroom Lasagna with Béchamel Sauce

A meatless version of lasagna that is so satisfying you won't miss the meat.

Ingredients:

Olive oil

3 yellow onions – halved and sliced thinly

Salt and pepper

3-4 sprigs of thyme

4 T butter

2 lbs mixed mushrooms – sliced (shiitake, brown button, mixed medley)

2 garlic cloves – sliced

1 bunch swiss chard – ribs removed, chopped

1/2 oz dried porcini mushrooms – soaked in 1/2 cup hot water, reserve liquid

3/4 lb Italian Fontina cheese – grated

1 cup parmesan – grated

1 package "no boil" lasagna noodles – soak in hot water for 15 minutes and drain

Béchamel Sauce:

3 T butter

3 T flour

1/3 cup mushroom liquid

3 cups milk – room temperature

1/2 tsp nutmeg

Preparation:

In large sauté pan over medium-low heat, add 2-3 T olive oil, sliced onions, salt and pepper to taste. Add fresh thyme, stir and cook for 10-15 minutes until browned and caramelized. Set aside. In large sauté pan over medium-high heat, add 2 T olive oil, 2 T butter and 1/2 the sliced mushrooms along with the garlic. Cook and stir until mushrooms are soft. Set aside. Repeat with remaining mushrooms adding olive oil and butter as needed. Next, sauté swiss chard with olive oil until soft, about 3-5 minutes. Combine onions, mushrooms, swiss chard and set aside.

For béchamel sauce, melt butter in a large sauté pan over medium heat. Add flour and cook for 2 minutes stirring constantly. Add mushroom liquid from dried mushrooms. Stir quickly then slowly whisk in milk. Continue to cook and stir until somewhat thickened, 10-15 minutes. Add nutmeg.

Preheat oven to 375 degrees. Assemble lasagna in a 9 x 13 inch dish. Scoop a 1/2 cup béchamel sauce and pour on bottom of pan. Next lay 4 noodles (no overlap), add another 1/2 to 3/4 cup of sauce and spread over noodles in a thin layer. Add 2 large spoonfuls of mushroom, onion and chard mixture, distributing evenly over sauce. Sprinkle 1/4 cup parmesan and 1 cup of fontina cheese. Repeat the process 3 more times and finish with cheese on top. Cover with parchment, then foil, and bake for 30-35 minutes. Uncover and bake for 10 more minutes. Let rest before serving. **Serves 6-8.**

Serve with:

Kunde Family Winery Merlot

Roasted Lemon Thyme Chicken with Baby Yukon Gold Potatoes

A classic and simple dish that will fill your kitchen with savory aromas as it cooks.

Ingredients:

5 lb chicken – wing tips removed

Salt and pepper

1 T fresh thyme

1 Meyer lemon – zested and quartered

1-2 lbs baby Yukon Gold potatoes

1 cup Chardonnay

Preparation:

Remove chicken from refrigerator 30 minutes before roasting and preheat oven to 500 degrees. In a mortar and pestle, place 1 T salt, thyme, lemon zest and crush together. Remove insides of chicken and use for stock another time. Sprinkle the cavity with the salt/thyme/lemon zest mixture. Place quartered lemon pieces inside the chicken. Salt and pepper the outside of the bird. Tie leg tips together with twine.

Place chicken in a 12 inch roasting pan, breast side up. Place potatoes all around chicken and sprinkle with salt and pepper. Place the roasting pan in the oven, legs first, and roast for 50 minutes or until the juices run clear. Tent with foil if browning too quickly. Tilt the chicken to drain juices into the pan and transfer the chicken to a serving platter. Tent with foil to keep warm.

Drain excess fat from drippings. Add the wine to the roasting pan and bring to a boil, scraping bits from the bottom of the pan. Continue cooking until reduced by half. Taste and add salt and pepper if needed. Serve chicken and potatoes with the sauce ladled over the top. **Serves 4-6.**

Serve with:

Kunde Family Winery Dunfillan Cuvée

"Baby Yukon Gold potatoes are so creamy. When topped with this sauce, they become even more tasty."

Nanny's Thanksgiving Turkey Stuffing with Sausage and Sage

My Grandmother Nanny made this stuffing every year for our family Thanksgiving dinner and part of the tradition was to use Jimmy Dean pork sausage.

Ingredients:

1 lb Jimmy Dean pork sausage

3/4 cup butter – divided

3 stalks celery – finely diced

1 large yellow onion – finely diced

2 cloves garlic – minced

Large handful of Italian leaf parsley – finely chopped

1 large bag Pepperidge Farms seasoned bread crumbs

2 eggs – beaten

1 tsp poultry seasoning

3-3 1/2 cups of chicken broth

Salt and pepper

Preparation:

In a large sauté pan, brown the sausage, breaking it into small pieces while it cooks and set aside in a bowl. Into the drippings, melt 1/4 cup butter. Add the celery, onion, garlic and parsley. Cook at medium-low heat for about 10 minutes, until vegetables are softened, stirring often. Remove from heat.

In a large bowl, add bread crumbs, eggs, sausage, vegetable mixture, 1/2 cup melted butter, poultry seasoning and mix to combine. Add 1 1/2 cups of the chicken broth, mixing to combine, followed slowly by the remaining broth, making sure the dressing is moist, not wet or dry. Season with salt and pepper to taste. When ready to cook your bird, stuff the turkey right before you put it in the oven. **Serves 6-8.**

Serve with:

Kunde Family Winery Malbec

Tip:

When adding liquid to the stuffing, remember that the moisture consistency when mixing in the broth will be the same consistency when you take it out of the turkey.

Apple and Walnut Stuffed Pork Chops with Cider Maple Glaze

Seared and roasted chops come alive with bold flavors and a rich sauce.

Ingredients:

4 thick cut pork chops – bone-in or boneless

Salt and pepper

Olive oil

1 yellow onion – thinly sliced

3 garlic cloves – chopped

2 fresh thyme sprigs

1 large Honey Crisp apple – quartered, cored and thinly sliced

3 T apple cider vinegar – divided

3 T maple syrup – divided

1/4 cup walnuts – toasted and chopped

1/4 cup chicken stock

1 T Dijon mustard

2 T butter

Preparation:

Make a generous horizontal slice in the side of each chop so there is room for a substantial amount of stuffing. Salt and pepper both sides of chop, rub with olive oil and set aside to make the stuffing.

In a large heavy skillet over medium heat, add 1-2 T of olive oil with the sliced onion. Sauté for 5-8 minutes, until onion slices are soft and caramelized. Add garlic, thyme, apple slices and a pinch of salt and pepper. Continue cooking for 3-5 minutes until apples soften. Add 1 T apple cider vinegar to deglaze pan and remove from heat. Add 1 T maple syrup and walnuts. Place mixture in bowl, set aside to cool and remove thyme sprigs.

Preheat oven to 400 degrees. To stuff pork chops, use about about 1/4 – 1/3 cup of filling per chop. Reserve remaining filling for sauce. In a clean heavy skillet over medium high heat, add 1-2 T of olive oil. When hot, add chops to pan and sear each side well, 3-5 minutes per side. Transfer skillet to oven and cook for 5 minutes. Check meat thermometer for internal temperature —145 degrees. Continue to cook if necessary. Remove from oven, transfer chops to a platter and cover with foil.

In same pan over medium heat, deglaze pan with remaining 2 T apple cider vinegar. Add chicken stock, Dijon mustard, and any remaining filling. Cook for 3-4 minutes. Add butter and the remaining 1-2 T maple syrup (depending on desired sweetness). Continue to cook and stir until butter is melted. Add salt and pepper to taste. Plate pork chops and drizzle sauce over the top. **Serves 4.**

Serve with:

Kunde Family Winery Syrah

Asian Fusion Beef Short Ribs

Oven braised short ribs with a rich Asian flavor influence.

Ingredients:

1 cinnamon stick

1 star anise

2 bay leaves

6 black peppercorns

4 juniper berries

5 cloves

1/2 teaspoon coriander seeds

Salt and pepper

4 lbs beef short ribs – rest at room temp for 30 minutes

Olive oil

1 large shallot – chopped

4 garlic cloves – chopped

2 inch piece of ginger – peeled

1 1/4 cups Cabernet Sauvignon

2-3 cups beef broth

1 T honey

1/4 cup soy sauce

1/2 cup hoisin sauce

Chopped scallions, toasted sesame seeds and cilantro for garnish

Preparation:

In a piece of cheese cloth, wrap up the cinnamon stick, anise, bay leaves, peppercorns, juniper berries, cloves, and coriander seeds. Trim excess fat and then salt and pepper the short ribs.

In a large Dutch oven over medium high heat, add 1-2 T of olive oil. When hot, add the short ribs in 2 batches and brown well on all sides. Remove to sheet pan. Add shallot, garlic and ginger to Dutch oven. Sauté for 2-4 minutes until brown. Deglaze pan with 1/4 cup red wine. Add remaining wine, beef broth, honey, soy sauce and hoisin sauce, followed by the short ribs. The ribs should be mostly submerged. If not, add more broth or water. Bring to a boil, add herbs in cheese cloth, cover and put in oven at 350 degrees for 1 hour. Then check and turn short ribs over. Resume cooking for 1 1/2 hours until meat easily pulls away from the bone with a fork.

Transfer meat to a serving platter and cover with foil to keep warm. Strain 1-2 cups sauce from pan and skim off as much fat as possible. Reduce if necessary. Serve the sauce over the ribs and garnish with scallions, sesame seeds and cilantro. Serve with steamed rice. **Serves 4.**

Serve with:

Kunde Family Winery Cabernet Sauvignon – Drummond

Hanger Steak Enchiladas

A great weeknight meal made even easier by using store bought enchilada sauce.

Ingredients:

1 3/4 lbs hanger steak

Salt and pepper

1 T taco seasoning

Olive oil

1 cup beef broth

3-4 yellow onions – thinly sliced

10-12 corn tortillas

1 jar enchilada sauce – 2-3 cups

2 red peppers – roasted, cut into thin strips

1 1/2 cups corn – fresh or frozen

2-3 cups jack cheese – shredded

Cilantro – chopped, for garnish

Scallions – chopped, for garnish

Sour cream

Preparation:

Generously season hanger steak with salt, pepper and taco seasoning. Leave at room temperature for 30 minutes. In Dutch oven over medium high heat, add olive oil and sear hanger steaks well on each side. Add 1 cup beef broth, cover, turn heat down and simmer, turning occasionally. Add more liquid if needed. This will take 1 1/2-2 hours. Let cool and shred. In a skillet over medium heat, add olive oil and caramelize the onions until golden, about 15-20 minutes. Set aside.

In another skillet, lightly warm tortillas on each side with a little oil or put on a sheet pan in the oven at 350 degrees for 5 minutes until warm and pliable.

To make the enchiladas, preheat oven to 400 degrees. Pour 1/3 cup enchilada sauce into a 9 x 13 inch baking dish. Cover each tortilla with sauce, a few tablespoons of meat, peppers, corn, cheese and then roll tortillas. Pour remaining sauce over the rolled enchiladas and finish with 1 cup of cheese. Bake for 25-30 minutes until cheese is melted and sauce is bubbling. Garnish with chopped cilantro, scallions and a dollop of sour cream. **Serves 4-6.**

Serve with:
Kunde Family Winery Zinfandel – Heritage Block

"Hamburger meat works equally well for this recipe. Brown meat in a saute pan with taco seasoning and salt and pepper. Set aside until ready to assemble the enchiladas."

Bacon Wrapped Filet Mignon with Port Reduction Sauce

Your taste buds will love the delectable meld of flavors and your eyes will delight with the exquisite presentation.

Ingredients:

3 T butter

2 T olive oil

1/2 lb shallots – whole and peeled

1 T sugar

1 cup Kunde Family Winery 1904 Dessert Cuvée

2 cups beef broth

Salt and pepper

4, 8 oz filet mignon

4 thick cut peppered bacon slices

8 oz cambozola cheese

Preparation:

Prepare the sauce first. In an oven proof pan, melt butter with olive oil and shallots. Add sugar and coat shallots well. Place in a 425 degree oven for 10-12 minutes or until shallots are very browned and caramelized. Toss twice while cooking. Remove from oven and deglaze pan with wine, reducing by half. Add beef stock, bring to a boil and then reduce heat to simmer for 1/2 hour or until thickened. Taste and adjust with salt and pepper if needed.

To prepare the filet, wrap 1 piece of bacon around each filet, securing with butcher twine. Grill the filet to desired doneness. Cut off twine and move filets to plates. Top each with a 2 oz wedge of cambozola. Pour heated sauce over the cheese to melt and serve immediately. **Serves 4.**

Serve with:
Kunde Family Winery Moon Mountain Red Wine

142

Pear Cranberry Crisps with Pecan Crumble Topping

All the fall flavors I love—pears, pecans, cranberries and cinnamon.

Ingredients:

5-6 Pears – Bosc, Anjou or both – peeled and cut into small pieces

2 tsp lemon zest

2 T lemon juice

1 1/4 cups fresh or frozen cranberries

1/2 tsp cinnamon

1-2 T maple syrup

Pinch of salt

Crumble Topping:

3/4 cup flour

1/2 cup brown sugar

1 cup pecans

1 1/2 sticks butter – cut into small chunks

1 tsp cinnamon

1/4 tsp nutmeg

1 cup oatmeal

Preparation:

Prepare crumble topping first. Combine flour, brown sugar and pecans in food processor and pulse 2-3 times. Add butter and pulse 2-3 more times until incorporated into pea size pieces. Add cinnamon, nutmeg, oatmeal and pulse 1-2 more times. Transfer mixture to a bowl, cover and place in refrigerator until ready to use.

Preheat oven to 375 degrees. To prepare the filling, in a medium bowl combine the pears, lemon zest, lemon juice, cranberries, cinnamon, maple syrup and a pinch of salt. Fill 6 small oven proof ramekins with the pear/cranberry filling. Top with crisp topping and place ramekins on a sheet pan and bake for 25-35 minutes until topping is brown. Check after 25 minutes. If topping is browning too quickly, turn down heat to 350 degrees and continue cooking until pears are soft. Cool and serve with vanilla ice cream or whipped cream. **Serves 6-8.**

Serve with:

Kunde Family Winery 1904 Dessert Cuvée

Tip:
If you prefer, you can easily prepare and serve this desert in an 8 x 8 inch dish instead of individual ramekins.

Gravenstein Apple Crumble Top Pie

If you're lucky enough to live where Gravenstein apples are grown, never miss a chance to bake with them. Tart, crisp, and firm—they offer amazing flavors.

Ingredients:

Pastry for 1 pie crust – I use Pillsbury Pie dough and it works perfectly

8 medium to large apples – Gravensteins or other firm apple

1/2 cup sugar

1 T flour

1 tsp cinnamon

1/4 tsp nutmeg

1/4 tsp salt

1 T lemon juice

Crumble Crust:

1 cup flour

3/4 cup sugar

1/2 cup butter – softened

1 tsp cinnamon

Preparation:

Preheat oven to 425 degrees. Line pie dish with the pastry. Peel, core and cut apples into thin slices. Place slices into a large bowl and add sugar, flour, spices and lemon juice. Mix the ingredients gently until the apple slices are well coated. Pour apples into the pie dish.

To prepare the crumble crust, in a medium bowl, place flour, sugar, butter and cinnamon. Rub together with your fingers or use a pastry cutter until the mixture clumps together. Heap the topping mixture on top of the apples. Place the pie pan on a foil covered baking sheet in case the juices spill over. Bake for 10 minutes at 425 degrees then reduce to 350 degrees and bake for an additional 50 minutes or until the apple mixture is bubbling and juicy. When serving, add a scoop of vanilla ice cream for an extra rich treat. **Serves 8.**

Serve with:

Kunde Family Winery Sweet Leslie

Tip:
If you're a cinnamon lover like I am, you can be overly generous with the cinnamon on the apples and in the crumble topping.

Zabaglione with Fall Fruit Compote

This Italian inspired custard is creamy and full-flavored with a rich, spicy topping of fall fruits.

Ingredients:

6 large egg yolks	1/4 cup golden raisins
1/4 cup sugar	1/4 cup dried figs – chopped
1/2 cup Marsala wine	2 T Kunde Family Winery 1904 Dessert Cuvée
Fruit Compote:	1/4 tsp ground cinnamon
1 T butter	1/8 tsp allspice
2 Bosc Pears - peeled and cut into 1/2 inch chunks	1 tsp honey
	2 tsp lemon juice
1/4 cup dried cranberries	1 tsp lemon zest

Preparation:

Prepare double boiler with low simmering water. Place the egg yolks and sugar in a large stainless bowl over double boiler. Don't let the bowl touch the water. Whip the yolks with a whisk over heat until they are pale yellow and creamy. Add the Marsala, whisking constantly until the mixture has formed soft mounds, about 10-15 minutes. Spoon into individual serving cups and refrigerate for 4-6 hours.

To prepare the fruit compote, melt butter in a small pan over medium heat. Add pears, cranberries, raisins, figs, 1904 Dessert Cuvée, spices, honey and cook for 5-10 minutes, until pears soften a bit. Add lemon juice, zest and combine well. Place in a serving bowl to cool. Serve on top or alongside Zabaglione. **Serves 4.**

Serve with:
Kunde Family Winery Sweet Leslie

"This wine was named after my Mom and the label needed to be extra special. To inspire the designer I showed him a ring of my Mom's that I wear everyday. Solid and feminine, a description that perfectly suits my beloved Mom."

Tip:
This dessert can be served either warm or cold in individual clear glasses on a handsome tray. Very festive!

Blessing of the grapes 1990

Harvest time fun!

Mom & Dad
Thanksgiving
Feast 1991

Winter

Every season in wine country brings its own beauty, even the grey skies of winter. The warmth of autumn gives way to chilly days filled with rain, soaking the volcanic rust red soils with its glorious moisture. The patchwork of grapevines that crisscross the valley floor and hillsides begin to shut down, leaving behind their canopy of canes after the rush of harvest. The wines linger in their slumber in the expanse of our aging caves, nestled in toasty oak barrels, anticipating the first calls of the bottling line. And in our homes, the scintillating aromas of savory soups and stews and favorite beloved holiday traditions await the gathering of family and friends.

Making Memories at Home

After the rush of harvest, the vineyards begin to quiet and then the hustle and bustle of the holidays arrive. While the 'elves' are busy in our Tasting Room shipping wines around the world for holiday enjoyment, the Kunde's prepare for delightful Christmas celebrations and traditions. A generation ago, the entire Kunde family would get together at the homestead house on the ranch for a large, boisterous gathering on Christmas Eve. Christmas morning was always my Mom and Dad's most favorite day of the year—we treasure our memories of them surprising us with a pony from Santa and my Dad indulging my Mom with a beautiful trinket every year.

What do I cherish most about Christmas? It's the feeling of peace and togetherness the holiday brings. Now with two grandchildren of our own, we relish in sharing the traditions that my husband and I grew up with—from decorating our home and trimming the tree to the foods that are so lovingly prepared and served to family and friends.

My brother Jeff's family photos on the upper and lower left. Middle picture on the left is all of the Kunde grandchildren with Big Boy and Honey on Christmas Eve. That cute little girl in the red dress on the right is me. Top right, 5th generation at Kunde Christmas Party. My two children in three bottom right photos.

Mom's Christmas Breakfast Casserole

A fabulous make-ahead breakfast for festive holiday gatherings.

Ingredients:

1/2 cup butter

1/2 lb fresh mushrooms – sliced

2 cups yellow onions – chopped

1 1/2 lbs mild Italian sausage

12 slices white bread – crusts removed

1/2 lb cheddar cheese – grated

1/2 lb Monterey Jack cheese – grated

5 eggs

2 1/2 cups whole milk

3 tsp Dijon mustard

1 tsp dry mustard

1 tsp ground nutmeg

Salt and pepper

2 T fresh parsley – finely chopped

Preparation:

Melt 1/2 cup butter, brown mushrooms and onions over medium heat until tender. Cook sausage and cut into bite size pieces. Grease 9 x 13 inch shallow casserole. Layer 1/2 the bread, mushroom mixture, sausage and cheese. Repeat layers, ending with cheese. Mix eggs, milk, both mustards, nutmeg, salt and pepper to taste. Pour over the sausage and cheese casserole. Cover and refrigerate overnight. Overnight is a must! When ready to bake, sprinkle the parsley over the top of the casserole and bake uncovered in preheated 350 degree oven for 1 hour or until bubbly. Serve immediately (or when finished opening Christmas presents!). **Serves 8-10.**

"My Mom would always make this delicious casserole Christmas day. After presents were opened, we would devour it! This has become our family's tradition every Christmas morning."

A few tips I've learned over the years for great holiday entertaining:

- I love the scent and look of fresh boughs of greenery on the table and mantle—from pine boughs to olive branches. Throw fresh pomegranates, pears and red apples in a beautiful bowl on your dining room table and you have instant festive decor.

- Have an ample amount of decorative linens and placemats on hand that fit the season. You never know when a small tribe of your besties will descend for a get together!

- For a more formal dinner, I just love bringing out my Mom's and Grandmother's sterling silver and china pieces. A mixture of colored water goblets that coordinate with the china and a red and white wine glass at each table setting, makes for a stunning and heartfelt table.

- If you've got an upcoming dinner party, look for recipes that you can make ahead and have cooking in the oven while you toast to the season. A few of my go-tos are on these holiday pages.

- Wondering what to serve for an easy appetizer? Try a selection of local and European wedges of cheese (I usually have 3), fresh cut slices of small artisan salamis or foie gras, sliced apples or pears, green olives, and a small bowl of pepper spiced marcona almonds. Arrange all on a large white platter with herbs or greenery from your yard or garden. It may seem simple and basic but your guests will always devour an appetizing charcuterie plate.

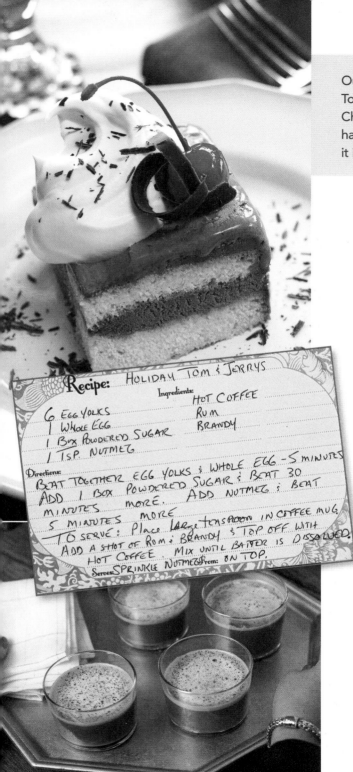

Our Mom would always make this ice cream cake for her holiday dinners. To continue the tradition, I make this cake now every year for our family's Christmas dinner. One infamous evening, my brother Jeff was so happy I had made this cake that he proudly spouted, "This cake is so awesome, it is better than sex!" I think wine might have been involved!!!

Chocolate Charlotte

Ingredients:

1 large container dark chocolate ice cream – softened

1 pre-made pound cake – completely cooled (I use Dromedary brand)

About 1 cup (give or take) dry sherry

Fresh sweetened whipped cream

Maraschino cherries with stem attached – dried on a paper towel

Shaved dark chocolate curls

Preparation:

You'll make this ice cream cake in an 8 x 8 inch shallow casserole style dish. Thinly slice the pound cake so that you'll have enough to cover the casserole dish 2 times. Arrange slices of the pound cake to cover the entire surface. Sprinkle the sherry heavily over the pound cake slices. Give it a pretty good soaking, but not soggy. Spread 1/2 of the ice cream of the top of the pound cake, making a smooth layer. Repeat with another layer of pound cake, sprinkle the sherry, and finish with another layer of chocolate ice cream. Seal it tight with saran wrap and put away in the freezer to harden. Should be made at least one day in advance. When you're ready to serve, cut the cake into squares and garnish with a dollop of whipped cream, a maraschino cherry, and chocolate curls.

Bob Kunde holding a Tom and Jerry

159

Mini Crab Cakes with Citrus Aioli

Delightful with fresh Pacific Dungeness Crab.

Ingredients:

2 1/2 cups cleaned crab meat – from 2 cooked crabs

1/2 cup panko

1 egg – whisked

1/4 cup mayonnaise

2 scallions – minced

1/4 cup cilantro – chopped

1/4 cup parsley – chopped

1 T mint – chopped

1 T lemon zest

1 T lemon juice – fresh

1/2 tsp old bay seasoning

1 tsp worcestershire sauce

1/4 tsp salt

1/4 tsp pepper

Olive oil

Citrus Aioli:

1/2 cup mayonnaise

1/4 tsp orange zest

1/2 tsp lemon zest

1 tsp mint – chiffonade

1 tsp lemon juice

Preparation:

Combine all citrus aioli ingredients in bowl and reserve in refrigerator until ready to serve.

Place all ingredients for the crab cakes in large bowl, except crab meat. Mix well, gently stir in crab meat. Shape mixture into 3/4 inch round cakes and place on tray, should make 12-14. In a skillet, heat 2 T olive oil then add the cakes. Cook until brown about 3-4 minutes, turn and cook another 3-4 minutes. Place on warm platter and serve immediately with citrus aioli. **Serves 3-4.**

Serve with:

Kunde Family Winery Magnolia Lane Sauvignon Blanc

"Not only delicious, but simple to make and a crowd pleaser."

Melted Brie and Sun Dried Tomatoes in Garlic Sourdough

This is such a simple recipe that is super easy to make for a large crowd.
Your guests will end up eating the entire bread bowl!

Ingredients:

1 seeded, round sourdough

2 T olive oil

3 cloves garlic – pressed

1 or 2 wheels of Brie cheese
(depending on the size of the loaf and the amount of people you are serving)

6-8 oz container prepared pesto sauce

1/2 cup sundried tomatoes – chopped (you can also use oil packed)

Baguette slices or water crackers

Preparation:

Remove top of sourdough round and scoop out the inside to create a bowl in the bread. Brush the olive oil around the entire inside surface of the bread and rub in the garlic cloves. Horizontally slice the top off the first wheel of Brie and place in the bread. Place a layer of the pesto sauce on top of the Brie. Horizontally slice the top off the 2nd wheel of Brie and place on top of the pesto. Layer the sundried tomatoes on top. Cover the bowl with aluminum foil and place in a 325°F oven for approximately 30 minutes. The cheese needs to be heated all the way through. Lay the seeded top at an angle on the bowl and serve with baguette slices or water crackers. **Serves 6-8.**

Serve with:
Kunde Family Winery Chardonnay

Crab Wontons with Sesame Soy Dipping Sauce

Created by Katy Long, wife of Kunde Winemaker Zach Long.

Ingredients:

1 cup (about 1/2 pound) Dungeness crab meat, shell pieces removed

2 tsp chives – sliced thinly

1/2 tsp lemon zest

1/2 tsp ginger – grated or finely minced

1/4 cup cream cheese – softened

Salt and pepper

24 wonton wrappers

1 egg lightly beaten with 1 tsp of water

Vegetable oil for frying (3 to 4 cups)

Sesame Soy Dipping Sauce:

1/3 cup soy sauce or tamari

2 T toasted sesame oil

2 T seasoned rice vinegar

1 tsp honey

1 tsp chili garlic sauce

Preparation:

To prepare dipping sauce whisk all ingredients in a small bowl and set aside.

Place cleaned crab meat in bowl and combine with chives, lemon zest, ginger and cream cheese. Mix until combined, adding salt and pepper to taste. On a dry cutting board lay out wonton skins. Put a teaspoon of filling on the center of each wrapper. Wet 2 edges of the wrapper with egg wash. Fold the corner of the wrapper to its opposite end to make a triangle shape, pressing edges to seal.

Heat frying oil on medium to medium high (350 degrees is desirable). Test oil with an unused wonton skin or edge of a wonton. If it bubbles, oil is ready. Fry in small batches until golden brown. Dry on paper towels. Serve wontons piping hot with Sesame Soy Dipping Sauce. **Serves 6-8.**

Serve with:

Kunde Family Winery Reserve Chardonnay

Prosciutto Wrapped Baby Potatoes with a Dijon Drizzle

I love baby red potatoes and prosciutto! A simple recipe for any size crowd.

Ingredients:

15-20 baby red potatoes

10 slices prosciutto – halved lengthwise

1-2 T olive oil

Dijon Drizzle:

1 T white wine vinegar

2 tsp Dijon mustard

1-2 tsp lemon juice

1-2 tsp lemon zest

1 tsp honey

1 garlic clove – crushed

1 tsp thyme leaves – chopped

1/4 cup olive oil

Salt and pepper

Preparation:

Put potatoes in a double boiler with water and steam for 10-15 minutes until just tender. Let cool slightly. Wrap each potato with half a slice of prosciutto and set on sheet pan. Drizzle with olive oil and roast for 10-20 minutes until golden and prosciutto is slightly crisp around edges.

While potatoes are cooking, make Dijon drizzle by combining all ingredients and whisking together. Taste and adjust seasoning if necessary. Spoon over potatoes and serve immediately. **Serves 4-6.**

Serve with:
Kunde Family Winery Red Dirt Red

ESTABLISHED 1904
KUNDE
FAMILY WINERY
Sonoma Valley
RED DIRT RED
ESTATE GROWN
Destination Series

Crab Salad with Tangerines and Ruby Beets

Fresh pomegranate seeds are a must for flavor and a beautiful burst of color.

Ingredients:

1 head butter lettuce or mixed greens – 5-6 cups

1 green apple – quartered and thinly sliced

1/2 fennel bulb – thinly sliced or shaved on mandoline

1 lb crab meat

4 tangerines or tangelos – zest 1 tsp
(then skin and section) save all juice for dressing

4 baby red beets – steamed or roasted

1/4 cup fresh mint – chiffonade

1/4 cup fresh pomegranate seeds

Fresh dill for garnish

Citrus Dressing:

1/4 cup freshly squeezed tangerine juice

1 tsp tangerine zest

1 tsp lemon juice

1 tsp honey

1/3 cup olive oil

Salt and pepper

Preparation:

Mix all dressing ingredients in a small bowl except olive oil. Slowly whisk in olive oil and salt and pepper to taste.

In a salad bowl, gently toss lettuce with apple, fennel, a little dressing and a pinch of salt and pepper. Next layer crab, tangerines, beets, mint, pomegranate seeds, dill and drizzle with more dressing to taste. This salad can be individually plated or served from a large salad bowl. Serves 4-6.

Serve with:

Kunde Family Winery Chardonnay – Wildwood Vineyard

Tip:
Crack the crab the night before to make the prep for this salad a snap.

Roasted Brussel Sprout Salad with Apples, Bacon and Toasted Pecans

Great texture and layers of flavor.

Ingredients:

1 lb brussel sprouts – washed and trimmed

2 T olive oil

Salt and pepper

1/2 cup pecans – toasted and chopped

3 slices bacon – cut into 1/2 inch pieces

1 Honey Crisp or other firm apple – sliced thin

Dressing:

1/4 cup olive oil

1 T apple cider vinegar

Small drizzle of honey

1-2 tsp of lemon juice

Preparation:

Thinly slice/shave brussel sprouts with sharp knife or mandolin. Toss with 2 T olive oil, salt, pepper and roast in oven at 400 degrees for 8-12 minutes until slightly caramelized and just beginning to turn brown. Remove from oven and set aside to cool slightly. At the same time brussel sprouts are roasting, toast pecans for 5-7 minutes. Cook chopped bacon over medium heat until crisp. Whisk together all ingredients for dressing, add salt and pepper to taste and set aside.

To assemble salad, place brussel sprouts on a platter. Add apple, bacon, pecans and drizzle with dressing. Gently toss and serve immediately. **Serves 4.**

Serve with:

Kunde Family Winery Sauvignon Blanc – Block 4SB20

Penne and White Bean Soup with Italian Sausage and Fresh Spinach

Warm and savory on a cold winter's night.

Ingredients:

1 yellow onion – peeled and diced

3 cloves garlic – peeled and pressed

4 large mild Italian pork sausage links

2 1/2 cups low sodium chicken broth

8 oz can tomato sauce

15 oz can diced tomatoes

1/2 cup red wine

1 tsp dried oregano

1 T dried basil

1 1/2 cups dried penne pasta

1 bunch fresh spinach leaves – washed and coarsely chopped

2, 15 oz cans white or cannellini beans – drained and rinsed

Salt and pepper

Parmesan cheese – freshly grated

Tip:
Toasted fresh sourdough bread or baked bread sticks are a nice complement to this steamy soup.

Preparation:

In a large pot over medium heat, sauté onion and garlic with olive oil, stir often for about 5 minutes. Add sausage and cook until no longer pink, breaking into bite sized pieces as it cooks. Add chicken broth, tomato sauce, diced tomatoes, red wine, spices, and penne pasta along with 1 1/2 cups of water. Stirring often, bring to a high simmer. Reduce heat a bit and cook until pasta is al dente, about 10-12 minutes.

Add spinach to the soup along with the white beans. Add a little more water if the mixture is too thick. Stir until all is heated through, about 5 minutes. Season to taste with salt and pepper. Serve in individual soup bowls and sprinkle the parmesan cheese over the top. **Serves 6-8.**

Serve with:

Kunde Family Winery Merlot

I make this recipe every year for Christmas Eve dinner. We like to serve this chowder alongside our other family tradition "Big Boy's Crab." I crafted our dining room table from reclaimed barn wood from the original Kinneybrook barn that stood where the winery now stands. As we gather around this table, with Kunde wine, we have the perfect recipe for a holiday gathering!

~ *Jeff Kunde*

Jeff's Christmas Eve Clam Chowder

Ingredients:

1/2 stick of butter

8, 8 oz bottles of clam juice

10, 6.5 oz cans of minced clams

8, 15 oz cans of cream of potato soup

3-4 red potatoes – cut into 1/2 inch cubes

4 stalks celery – chopped

1 bunch parsley – chopped

1 white onion – chopped

1 package thick cut bacon – cut into 1 inch slices

Worcestershire sauce – 6 dashes

Tabasco sauce – 4 dashes

Preparation:

Melt the butter in a large heavy stock pot. Pour the eight bottles of clam juice into the pot. Add canned clams with their juice, all cans of cream of potato soup and bring to a simmer. Add the potatoes, celery, parsley and onion. Bring pot back to a simmer and cover.

In a frying pan, sauté bacon until crispy. Drain all but 2 T of bacon drippings. Add bacon and drippings to soup and stir. Reduce heat and cover. Stir every 20 minutes or turn off the heat periodically to avoid burning. Season with worcestershire and tobasco. **Serves 8-10.**

Serve with:
Kunde Family Winery Chardonnay

Pork Pozole

A fun dish to serve family style—assorted toppings let everyone make it their own.

Ingredients:

2 T olive oil

2 lbs pork shoulder – trimmed, cut into 1 inch pieces and salted

1 onion – chopped

3 garlic cloves – chopped

3-4 cups chicken broth

2 cups hominy – drained and rinsed or 1 cup dried, soaked and cooked

2 tsp dried oregano

2 bay leaves

3 dried red New Mexico chilies – stemmed and seeded

1/4 cup cilantro – chopped

2 T lime juice

Salt

Toppings:

1 avocado – chopped

2 cups green cabbage – shredded

4 scallions – thinly sliced

5 radishes – thinly sliced

2 limes – cut into wedges

1 jalapeño – thinly sliced

Preparation:

In a 6 quart stock pot over medium heat, add olive oil and pork pieces (in 2 separate batches). Cook until brown and set aside. Cook onion and 2 garlic cloves for 2-4 minutes until soft, adding more oil if necessary. Add pork, broth, hominy, oregano and bay leaves to pot and simmer over medium heat for 20 minutes. Spoon off any excess fat.

While pot is simmering, toast chilies in a skillet over medium heat for 30-45 seconds until soft. Transfer them to a bowl and cover with boiling water. Soak for 15 minutes until soft. In a blender, add chilies with a little soaking liquid, 1 clove garlic and a pinch of salt. Puree until smooth paste. Add chili puree to the pot and cook 5-10 more minutes. If too thick, add more liquid. Add chopped cilantro, lime juice, and salt to taste.

Serve family style with the serving pot of pozole in the middle of table or serve in individual bowls and let everyone garnish with their favorite toppings. **Serves 4-6.**

Serve with:
Kunde Family Winery Merlot

Glamour Boy!

Big Boy's Kunde Family Crab

Of all the culinary traditions of the Kunde Family, this recipe is the coup de grâce and has been handed down to each generation from our Grandfather, Arthur "Big Boy" Kunde.

Ingredients:

5 Dungeness crabs

Marinade:

2 stalks celery

1/2 yellow onion

1/2 bunch of fresh Italian parsley

2 cloves garlic

1/4 cup olive oil

1/4 cup vegetable oil

1/4 cup apple cider vinegar

Juice of 2 lemons

1 lg tsp horseradish – prefer Beaver brand

Salt and pepper

Preparation:

Brush crab shells, rinse, crack and place in a large glass or wooden bowl. Finely chop the celery, onion, parsley and garlic. I use my Cuisinart to get a nice fine even chop.

Add the oils, vinegar, lemon juice, horseradish and pour over the cracked crab. Salt and pepper to taste.

Cover and put in the refrigerator, stirring every few hours. The longer it sits the better it gets! Serve alongside fresh sourdough French bread and you've got a traditional Kunde family meal. **Serves 4-6.**

Serve with:

Kunde Family Winery Chardonnay – Wildwood Vineyard

"I remember chopping for hours in my Mom's huge wooden bowl to get the dice just right on the vegetables and garlic. Now with my trusty Cuisinart, it's a snap!"

Tip:
Make sure to prepare first thing in the morning and stir every couple of hours. Can also be made the day before.

180

Sonoma Seafood Cioppino

The wonderful flavors of the northern coast of California.

Ingredients:

3 T olive oil

1 1/2 cups yellow onion – chopped

1 cup fennel bulb – chopped

3 cloves garlic – chopped

3 bay leaves

1 tsp dried oregano

1/4 tsp crushed red pepper flakes
(more if you like it spicy)

1/2 tsp salt

1/2 tsp pepper

28 oz can crushed tomatoes

16 oz can petite cut tomatoes

8 oz bottle clam juice

1 1/2 cups Chardonnay

1 cup fresh Italian parsley – chopped

1 lb fresh halibut – cut into 1 1/2" pieces

1 lb small clams or mussels

1 lb fresh wild medium shrimp – shelled and deveined

1 fresh Dungeness crab – cracked and cleaned

1 T fresh lemon juice

Preparation:

Heat olive oil in a large heavy pot over medium heat. Add onion, fennel, garlic, bay leaves, oregano, red pepper flakes, salt and pepper. Cook until the onion is tender. Stir in tomatoes with juices, clam juice, wine, parsley, and 1 cup water. Cover, bring to a high simmer, then reduce heat to low and cook, stirring often, until flavors meld, about 15 minutes. Stir in halibut, clams or mussels, shrimp and bring back to a simmer. Cook for about 2 minutes. Add crab, cover, and cook until clams/mussels open and seafood is cooked through, about 5 minutes. Add a generous squeeze of lemon juice. Taste and adjust salt and pepper. Serve with crusty sourdough bread. **Serves 4-6.**

Serve with:

Kunde Family Winery Reserve Chardonnay

"I love serving this on a cold winter's night. Fresh seafood in a savory sauce served with sourdough french bread. Scrumptious."

Wild Duck Breast with Chili Glaze and Wild Rice

A succulent sauce that carries some heat, combined with a sweet finish.
A great recipe from my friend Mark.

Ingredients:

4 wild duck breasts

Salt and pepper

Long grain and wild rice – cooked and ready to serve

Chili Glaze:

1/2 cup seasoned rice vinegar

2 tsp red chili flakes – more if you like it hot

2 cloves garlic – minced

1 T sweet yellow onion – minced

3/4 cup light brown sugar

1 T tomato paste

1/3 cup low sodium soy sauce

1/2 tsp kosher salt

1/4 cup butter

Preparation:

To prepare the glaze, bring the rice vinegar, chili flakes, garlic and onion to a medium simmer in a heavy sauce pot and reduce by half. Add the brown sugar, tomato paste, soy sauce, salt and bring it back to a full simmer for about 5 minutes. Remove from heat and whisk in the butter. Cover and keep warm to serve with the duck.

De-breast the wild duck and season the breasts with salt and pepper. Prepare your grill and place the duck breasts, skin side down, on the grill. Grill until the skin is crispy but not black. Turn the breasts over and grill for another 2 minutes or until the interior meat is light pink. Do not overcook! Remove from heat and cover with foil to keep warm until ready to serve.

When ready to plate, slice the duck breast thinly and serve over a bed of rice. Ladle a spoonful of the warm glaze over the top of the duck breast and serve immediately. **Serves 6-8.**

Serve with:
Kunde Family Winery Zinfandel

"My father was an avid duck hunter. He loved when my Mom would prepare fresh, wild duck that was cooked at a very high heat and then served rare. My mother would curse him for her super dirty oven every time she cooked his duck!"

Maple Pork Chops with Caramelized Figs and Fennel

Fresh figs and fennel bring this dish to life.

Ingredients:

4 pork chops

1-2 T olive oil

Salt and pepper

8-10 ripe figs – halved

2 small fennel bulbs – halved then sliced into 1/2 inch wedges

1 shallot – sliced

2 garlic cloves – chopped

2 T apple cider vinegar

1 T Dijon mustard

1/4 cup maple syrup

2 T butter

Tip:
Smashed or mashed potatoes would be a welcome side for this delicious dish, or get extra creative and add a yam.

Preparation:

Preheat oven to 400 degrees. Drizzle pork chops with olive oil and season with salt and pepper. In a large oven proof fry pan over medium high heat, add 1 T olive oil and sear pork on each side for 4-5 minutes. In a bowl, toss figs and fennel with a drizzle of olive oil. Add to the pork chops and roast in oven for 8-10 minutes until pork is done—145 degrees internal temp.

Remove pork, figs and fennel to a warm dish. Set aside and tent with foil. In same pan, add shallot, garlic and cider vinegar to deglaze the pan and loosen any bits of pork. Add Dijon and maple syrup. Whisk and continue to cook for a few more minutes then add the butter and whisk into a nice sauce. Add salt and pepper to taste. Immediately serve with pork, figs and fennel. **Serves 4.**

Serve with:
Kunde Family Winery Dunfillan Cuvée

Smoky Black Bean Chili

This picture says it all—soul warming!

Ingredients:

1 T olive oil or bacon fat

1 onion – chopped

2 garlic cloves – chopped

1 carrot – chopped

1 small jalapeño – seeded and chopped

1 1/2 lbs ground beef

1 tsp smoked paprika

1 tsp cumin

1/2 tsp cinnamon

2 tsp dried oregano

1 chipotle chili in adobo sauce – seeded and chopped plus 2 tsp sauce (more to taste)

28 oz can fire roasted crushed tomatoes

2, 15 oz cans black beans – drained and rinsed

1 T molasses

1/2 cup chicken stock or water

Salt and pepper

2 limes for garnish

1/2 cup cilantro leaves for garnish

1/2 cup sour cream for garnish

Preparation:

In large soup pot over medium heat, add 1 T oil or bacon fat and sauté onion, garlic cloves, carrot and jalapeño for 5 minutes. Add the ground beef and continue cooking for 5 more minutes then add the spices, chipotle sauce and chili. Continue cooking until meat is done, then add tomatoes and black beans. Continue simmering another 20 minutes to allow flavors to blend. Add the molasses and check for consistency. If too thick, add stock or water. Taste for desired smoky flavor and spice, adding more chipotle sauce, molasses and salt and pepper if needed. Serve immediately with fresh lime wedges, cilantro and sour cream or any other favorite chili toppings. **Serves 6.**

Serve with:

Kunde Family Winery Zinfandel

Tip:

If using dry black beans (worth the extra effort for flavor and texture), rinse and soak 1 1/2 cups overnight. In large stockpot over medium high heat, add 1 T of desired fat—using the bacon fat will add a lot of flavor. Sauté 1 chopped onion and 2 garlic cloves for 2-3 minutes. Add black beans drained of all soaking liquid to pot and cover with water 1-2 inches above the beans. Continue cooking over medium high heat, simmering for 1-1 1/2 hours until beans are tender, adding more water as necessary to keep water above beans while cooking.

ESTABLISHED 1904
KUNDE
FAMILY WINERY
Sonoma Valley
ZINFANDEL
WINERY BOND NO. 202
ESTATE GROWN

Savory Braised Beef Brisket with Zesty Gremolata

Use Meyer lemons as they are sweet and flavorful. You can also make this brisket in your crockpot.

Ingredients:

2-3 lbs brisket (room temperature for 1/2 hour-1 hour before cooking)

Salt and pepper

2 T olive oil

1 onion – chopped

1 carrot – chopped

1 celery – chopped

2 garlic cloves – chopped

2 1/3 cups dry red wine – divided

3-4 cups beef stock

1 1/2 cups diced tomatoes

Zesty Gremolata:

2 T olive oil

2 garlic cloves – chopped

Lemon zest

1/2 cup parsley – chopped

Salt and pepper

Bouquet Garni:

1 sprig rosemary

2 bay leaves

5 sprigs parsley

5 sprigs thyme

Preparation:

Generously salt and pepper brisket. In a heavy pot over medium high heat, add 2 T olive oil. When hot, add brisket and sear well on all sides and ends. Rest meat on sheet pan. Add chopped onion, carrot, celery and 2 garlic cloves to the pot. Saute for 3-5 minutes and then deglaze with 1/3 cup red wine. Place brisket on vegetables and add 3 cups of beef stock, 2 cups of red wine and tomatoes. Add bouquet garni and bring to a boil for 2-3 minutes. Place lid on the pot and cook for 3-4 hours at 350 degrees. After one hour, turn meat over and continue to cook.

To make gremolata, heat 2 T olive oil, remaining 2 garlic cloves and heat in small sauté pan. When garlic begins to sizzle, remove from heat and set aside to cool. In a medium bowl, place zest of lemon, chopped parsley, pinch of salt and pepper and mix together. Add garlic olive oil, squeeze of lemon juice and combine in bowl. Set aside to serve on top of brisket as garnish.

After 2 1/2 hours check to make sure there is enough liquid in the pot. Add 1-2 cups of beef stock as needed. Continue to cook until meat is tender and falls apart. Remove bouquet garni and set meat on sheet pan. Cover with foil. Skim excess fat off sauce and discard. If sauce needs thickening, reduce over high heat or add 2 T corn starch, pre-mixed with water to avoid lumps. Salt and pepper to taste. Slice brisket and serve immediately with sauce and gremolata. Serve with mashed potatoes or polenta. **Serves 4**.

Serve with:

Kunde Family Winery Red Dirt Red

Red Wine Infused Beef Stroganoff with Mushroom Medley

You'll impress your guests with this easy to prepare hearty meal.

Ingredients:

1 1/2 lbs beef tenderloin or sirloin steak	1/3 cup dry red wine
Salt and pepper	2 T flour
2 T butter	1 1/2 cups beef broth
2 T olive oil	1 T Dijon mustard
1 onion – thinly sliced	1 cup sour cream
1 lb mixed mushrooms – quartered	1/4 cup dill – chopped
3 fresh thyme sprigs	1 lb egg noodles – cooked per package directions

Preparation:

Cut meat into 2 inch thin strips and season with salt and pepper. Heat butter in large skillet and brown meat in 2 batches. Set aside meat and juices in bowl. In same pan, add olive oil and onion. Sauté 3-5 minutes over medium heat until soft. Turn up heat to medium high and add 1-2 T olive oil or butter. Add mushrooms, thyme and cook until soft 5-7 minutes.

Reduce heat to medium and add red wine to deglaze pan. Add flour to thicken sauce and stir well. Add broth, stir well and continue to cook for 8-10 minutes. Add meat and Dijon mustard and simmer for 3-5 minutes longer. Remove from heat, stir in sour cream, 1 T dill and mix well. Serve over egg noodles and garnish with an additional tablespoon of sour cream and remaining dill. **Serves 4-6.**

Serve with:

Kunde Family Winery Meritage 202

"I love cooking this satisfying beef dish for my husband. Beef, noodles, sour cream and a great bottle of wine. Always puts a smile on his face on a cold winter's night"

Cabernet Sauvignon Braised Short Ribs

This is an incredibly savory dish that is sure to please. Put it in your crock pot and come home to a delicious hot meal.

Ingredients:

5 lbs bone-in beef short ribs – leaner the better

Salt and pepper

1-2 T olive oil

3 medium onions – chopped

3 medium carrots – peeled and chopped

3 T flour

2 T tomato paste

1 bottle Cabernet Sauvignon

1 T Better than Bouillon beef base – a concentrated beef stock

4 cups low sodium beef broth

1 head of garlic – halved crosswise

Bouquet Garni:

10 sprigs flat-leaf parsley

8 sprigs thyme

4 sprigs oregano

2 sprigs rosemary

2 dried bay leaves

Preparation:

Season short ribs with salt and pepper. Heat oil in a large fry pan over medium-high heat and brown short ribs on all sides in a couple of batches. Transfer the short ribs to a crock pot. Leave about 2 T of the fat drippings in the pan. Add onions and carrots to the pan and cook over medium heat, stirring often, until softened, about 7 minutes. Add flour and tomato paste to the pan, incorporating into the vegetables. Cook, stirring constantly until well combined and deep red, about 3 minutes. Stir in Cabernet (yes – a whole bottle!), followed by the beef bouillon and broth. Bring to a boil and then pour over top of ribs in the crock pot. Prepare a bouquet garni with the parsley, thyme, oregano, rosemary and bay leaves. Add the garlic halves along with the herbs to the crock pot, laying on top of the liquid surface.

Cook until short ribs are tender, usually 8 hours in your crock pot. Spoon fat from surface of sauce and discard. Season sauce to taste with salt and pepper. Serve short ribs and sauce in shallow bowls over mashed potatoes. **Serves 4-6.**

Serve with:
Kunde Family Winery Reserve Cabernet Sauvignon

Tip:
I prepare this the night before, put it all in my crockpot, place in the fridge and then just plug it in on my way out the door in the morning.

Winter Fruit Crisp

A change of pace from a traditional summer fruit crisp.

Ingredients:

1 1/2 cups dry red wine

1/4 cup honey

1/4 cup maple syrup

1 cinnamon stick

1 bay leaf

3 cardamom pods

3 whole allspice

1 cup dried figs – cut into 4 to 6 wedges

4 Bosc or other firm pears – peeled, cored and cut into 1/2 inch pieces

4 apples, Granny Smith or other firm apple – peeled, cored and cut into 1/4 inch pieces

1/2 cup dried cranberries

Crisp Topping:

1 cup flour

1 cup oats

1/2 cup light brown sugar

1 tsp cinnamon

Pinch of salt

1 stick plus 3 T butter – cut into chunks

1/2 cup walnuts – optional

Preparation:

Make crisp topping by combining flour, oats, sugar, cinnamon and salt in a medium bowl. With your fingers, rub the butter chunks into the flour mixture until butter is well incorporated and small crumbs form. Add nuts if using and mix in. Chill topping while making the fruit mixture.

In sauce pan bring wine, honey, maple syrup and spices to a boil. Reduce heat to medium low and simmer uncovered for 8-10 minutes. Skim any foam. Add figs, pears, apples and simmer gently until pears are tender 5-8 minutes. Remove fruit and spices to a small bowl and discard spices. Return wine to medium-high heat and reduce to a thick syrup, about 10-15 minutes.

Preheat oven to 375 degrees. In a shallow 3 quart greased baking dish, add figs, pears, apples, cranberries, reduced wine syrup and gently toss until combined. Sprinkle crisp topping evenly over top. Bake for 30-40 minutes until topping is brown and juices are bubbling. Serve warm with ice cream or whipped cream. **Serves 6-8.**

Serve with:

Kunde Family Winery 1904 Dessert Cuvée

EST.

·1904·

Dessert Cuvée

KUNDE
FAMILY ESTATE

Baked Pears in Zinfandel and Dessert Cuvée Glaze

Simply delectable with a truly elegant presentation.

Ingredients:

2 cups Zinfandel

1 cup Kunde Family Winery 1904 Dessert Cuvée

1 cup sugar

1 cinnamon stick

2 inch piece of lemon and orange zest

8 Bosc pears – ripe but firm with stems attached

Fresh mint leaves

Preparation:

Preheat oven to 350 degrees. In a medium non-aluminum saucepan over medium heat, bring all ingredients, excluding pears and mint, to a simmer and dissolve the sugar. Remove the cinnamon stick. Core the pears from the bottom and then cut the bottom flat so that they can stand upright. Place the pears in a large baking pan (upright) and pour wine mixture over them. Bake for about an hour or until pears are tender when pierced with a knife, basting every 15 minutes with the wine mixture. Remove pears from the oven and pour off remaining mixture into a medium saucepan. Reduce the wine until it becomes a glaze. Spoon the glaze over the pears. Garnish with mint leaves and serve warm with ice cream if desired. These pears are also excellent served at room temperature. **Serves 8.**

Serve with:

Kunde Family Winery 1904 Dessert Cuvée

"From my friend Paige – an incredible cook!"

Tip:

For an extra special treat, drizzle with a dark chocolate sea salt glaze. Stonewall Kitchen is our favorite!

Chocolate Raspberry Brownies

A different twist on decadent brownies—add fresh raspberries!

Ingredients:

1 1/2 cups butter

12 oz semi sweet chocolate chips – divided

3 eggs

1 tsp vanilla

1 1/4 cups sugar

1 3/4 cups flour

1/2 tsp baking powder

2 cups raspberries – divided

Preparation:

Preheat oven to 350 degrees. Grease and flour 8 inch pan. Melt butter with 8 oz chocolate chips in sauce pan over low heat, stirring well until melted and set aside. In a large bowl, whisk eggs, vanilla and sugar until well blended and thick. Add melted chocolate slowly, mixing to incorporate.

In a small bowl, combine flour, baking powder and add to egg/chocolate mixture, stirring until smooth. Fold in 1 cup raspberries and half the remaining chocolate chips. Pour into prepared baking dish, then sprinkle the remaining berries and chocolate chips around the top. Bake for 45-55 minutes or until a toothpick comes out clean. Let cool and serve. **Serves 10-12.**

Serve with:

Kunde Family Winery Reserve Century Vines Zinfandel

Tip:
Fresh raspberries
might be hard to find
in the winter, but
frozen just won't do.

Chocolate Pumpkin Ricotta Cheesecake with a Chocolate Wafer Crust

The addition of chocolate and ricotta are a great variation from the traditional pumpkin cheesecake.

Ingredients:

1 cup pumpkin – strained of any liquid

1 tsp vegetable oil

10 oz quality semisweet chocolate

2, 12 oz containers ricotta cheese

1 tsp cinnamon

1/4 tsp ginger

1/4 tsp nutmeg

1/8 tsp cloves

1/8 tsp allspice

3/4 cup heavy cream – whipped

2 packages chocolate wafers – 10 oz each

Semisweet chocolate shavings for garnish

Preparation:

Strain pumpkin in a fine mesh strainer until all liquid is gone. Pumpkin should be thick. Prepare 9-inch round spring form pan by placing parchment paper on the bottom and sides of pan. Spray or use thin brush to coat with oil. Melt chocolate and set aside to cool. Place ricotta cheese in large bowl and blend until smooth. Add melted chocolate, pumpkin, spices and combine until smooth, scraping sides. In another bowl, whip cream until stiff peaks form and then gently fold into ricotta mixture.

To assemble, arrange half the cookies in a slightly over-lapping pattern to cover bottom of pan. Spoon half of the ricotta mixture evenly on top of cookies. Cover with the remaining cookies and top with remaining mixture, smooth top. Cover with plastic wrap and refrigerate at least 12 hours or up to 2 days. Release sides of pan and remove parchment paper. Using a metal spatula lift/slide cake and remove paper and set on serving platter. Shave chocolate over top of cake using a vegetable peeler. Use knife dipped in hot water to slice cake. **Serves 10-12.**

Serve with:
Kunde Family Winery 1904 Dessert Cuvée

Tip:
This is a great dessert to prepare ahead of your holiday gathering.

Daddy I see my bull!

Patiently waiting for our Christmas treats!

My Dad on Snowball
and his faithful
companion Toby

6th
generation
winemaker
in-training

Index

Dessert

Baked Pears in Zinfandel and Dessert Cuvee Glaze, 199
Chocolate Charlotte, 159
Chocolate Pumpkin Ricotta Cheesecake with a Chocolate Wafer Crust, 203
Chocolate Raspberry Brownies, 200
Gravenstein Apple Crumble Top Pie, 146
Leslie's Wine Cake, 46
Marinated Strawberries Divine, 95
Pear Cranberry Crisps with Pecan Crumble Topping, 145
Plum Berry Crumble, 99
Red Velvet Cake with Summer Berries, 100
Rustic Cherry Apricot Tart, 96
Springtime Strawberry Pie, 45
Strawberry Balsamic Tartlets, 42
Winter Fruit Crisp, 196
Zabaglione with Fall Fruit Compote, 149

Fruit

Apple, Caramelized, Salad with Blue Cheese, Walnuts and Dijon Dressing, 116
Apple, Gravenstein Crumble Top Pie, 146
Apple, Roasted Brussel Sprout Salad with Bacon and Toasted Pecans, 170
Apple, Walnut Stuffed Pork Chops with Cider Maple Glaze, 137
Apple, Winter Fruit Crisp, 196
Apricot, Grilled, Stuffed with Blue Cheese, Marcona Almonds and Parma Ham, 61
Apricot, Rustic Cherry Tart, 96
Avocado, Salad with Red Grapefruit, 19
Berries, Summer, Red Velvet Cake, 100
Berry, Plum Crumble, 99
Cherry, Rustic Apricot Tart, 96
Cranberry, Dried, Winter Fruit Crisp, 196
Cranberry, Fresh, Pear Crisps with Pecan Crumble Topping, 145

Fig, Salad with Fresh Ricotta, Honey Walnuts and Pomegranate Seeds, 112
Figs, Caramelized, Maple Pork Chops with Fennel, 187
Figs, Dried, Winter Fruit Crisp, 196
Grapefruit, Red, Salad with Avocado, 19
Mango, Fresh, Asian Noodle Salad with Beef Filet, 41
Peach, Grilled, Arugula Salad with Feta and Spicy Seed Brittle, 69
Pear, Baked, Zinfandel and Dessert Cuvée Glaze, 199
Pear, Caramelized Onion Crostini, 108
Pear, Cranberry Crisps with Pecan Crumble Topping, 145
Pear, Roasted, Harvest Salad with Blue Cheese and Balsamic Vinaigrette, 115
Pear, Winter Fruit Crisp, 196
Pear, Zabaglione, Fall Fruit Compote, 149
Plum, Berry Crumble, 99
Plum, Summer Beef Pizzettes, 84
Raspberry, Chocolate Brownies, 200
Sangria, Uncle Dick's, 54
Strawberry, Balsamic Tartlets, 42
Strawberry, Marinated Divine, 95
Strawberry, Spinach Salad with Marcona Almonds, 66
Strawberry, Springtime Pie, 45
Tangerines, Crab Salad with Ruby Beets, 169
Watermelon, Tomato Gazpacho, 65

Main Entrees

Apple and Walnut Stuffed Pork Chops with Cider Maple Glaze, 137
Asian Fusion Beef Short Ribs, 138
Asian Noodle Salad with Fresh Mango and Beef Filet, 41
Bacon Wrapped Filet Mignon with Port Reduction Sauce, 142
Big Boy's Kunde Family Crab, 180
Cabernet Sauvignon Braised Short Ribs, 195
Caprese Burger, 88

Caramelized Onion and Mushroom Lasagna with Béchamel Sauce, 130
Chicken Saltimbocca with Prosciutto and Fresh Sage, 34
Citrus Bok Choy, Shiitake Mushrooms and Beef Stir-Fry over Rice, 83
Grilled Chicken with Corn and Green Chili Salsa, 80
Grilled Lamb Chops with Pistachio Herb Sauce, 37
Grilled Portobello Sandwich with Caramelized Onions, Pesto Mayo and Balsamic Glaze, 27
Grilled Rib Eye Steaks with Caramelized Onions and Blue Cheese, 92
Halibut with Fennel, Olives and Cherry Tomatoes, 79
Hanger Steak Enchiladas, 141
Linguini with Fresh Baby Clams in a Chardonnay Infused White Sauce, 30
Maple Pork Chops with Caramelized Figs and Fennel, 187
Miso-Glazed Salmon with Shitake Mushroom Rice, 123
Mom's Christmas Breakfast Casserole, 157
Mushroom Risotto with Prawns and Saffron, 124
Nanny's Thanksgiving Turkey Stuffing with Sausage and Sage, 134
Pasta Vino, 129
Pork Satay with Cucumber Lettuce Wraps and Zesty Peanut Sauce, 38
Red Wine Infused Beef Stroganoff with Mushroom Medley, 192
Roasted Lemon Thyme Chicken with Baby Yukon Gold Potatoes, 133
Roasted Red Pepper and Hamburger Pizza with Smoked Mozzarella and Fresh Arugula, 87
Savory Braised Beef Brisket with Zesty Gremolata, 191
Skirt Steak with Red Chimichurri, 91
Smoky Black Bean Chili, 188
Sonoma Seafood Cioppino, 183
Sriracha Lime Grilled Fish Tacos, 74

Summer Beef and Plum Pizzettes, 84
Teriyaki Chicken with Savoy Cabbage and Scallions, 33
Wild Duck Breast with Chili Glaze and Wild Rice, 184

Lamb
Chops, Grilled, with Pistachio Herb Sauce, 37

Pasta
Capellini, Seafood Salad, 20
Lasagna, Caramelized Onion and Mushroom with Béchamel Sauce, 130
Linguini, Fresh Baby Clams in a Chardonnay Infused White Sauce, 30
Noodle, Asian Salad with Fresh Mango and Beef Filet, 41
Penne, White Bean Soup with Italian Sausage and Fresh Spinach, 173
Rigatoni, Pasta Vino, 129

Pork
Bacon, Crispy, Fresh Corn Chowder, 73
Bacon, Filet Mignon Wrapped with Port Reduction Sauce, 142
Bacon, Roasted Brussel Sprout Salad with Apples and Toasted Pecans, 170
Italian Sausage, Mom's Christmas Breakfast Casserole, 157
Italian Sausage, Pasta Vino, 129
Italian Sausage, Penne and White Bean Soup with Fresh Spinach, 173
Parma Ham, Grilled Apricots Stuffed with Blue Cheese and Marcona Almonds, 61
Pork Chops, Apple and Walnut Stuffed with Cider Maple Glaze, 137
Pork Chops, Maple with Caramelized Figs and Fennel, 187
Pork Satay, Cucumber Lettuce Wraps and Zesty Peanut Sauce, 38

Pork Shoulder, Pozole, 177
Prosciutto, Chicken Saltimbocca with Fresh Sage, 34
Prosciutto, Wrapped Baby Potatoes with a Dijon Drizzle, 166
Sausage, Nanny's Thanksgiving Turkey Stuffing with Sage, 134

Poultry
Chicken:
Chicken, Chinese Salad with Napa Cabbage and Toasted Sesame Seeds, 23
Chicken, Grilled with Corn and Green Chili Salsa, 80
Chicken, Roasted Lemon Thyme with Baby Yukon Gold Potatoes, 133
Chicken, Saltimbocca with Prosciutto and Fresh Sage, 34
Chicken, Teriyaki, with Savoy Cabbage and Scallions, 33
Chicken Wings, Asian with Shredded Cabbage Slaw, 16
Duck:
Duck Breast, Wild, with Chili Glaze and Wild Rice, 184
Turkey:
Thanksgiving Stuffing, Nanny's with Sausage and Sage, 134

Rice
Rice, Wild, Duck Breast with Chili Glaze, 184
Risotto, Mushroom with Prawns and Saffron, 124
Shiitake Mushroom, with Miso-Glazed Salmon, 123

Salads
Asian Flank Steak Salad, 24
Asian Noodle Salad with Fresh Mango and Beef Filet, 41
Caramelized Apple Salad with Blue Cheese, Walnuts and Dijon Dressing, 116
Chinese Chicken Salad with Napa Cabbage and Toasted Sesame Seeds, 23
Crab Salad with Tangerines and Ruby Beets, 169

Green Bean Salad with Baby Potatoes and Herb Dijon Vinaigrette, 70
Grilled Peach and Arugula Salad with Feta and Spicy Seed Brittle, 69
Red Grapefruit and Avocado Salad, 19
Roasted Brussel Sprout Salad with Apples, Bacon and Toasted Pecans, 170
Roasted Fig Salad with Fresh Ricotta, Honey Walnuts and Pomegranate Seeds, 112
Roasted Pear and Blue Cheese Harvest Salad with Balsamic Vinaigrette, 115
Seafood Capellini Salad, 20
Spinach Strawberry Salad with Marcona Almonds, 66

Sandwiches
Caprese Burger, 88
Grilled Portobello with Caramelized Onions, Pesto Mayo and Balsamic Glaze, 27

Seafood
Ahi, Poke Skewers, 58
Cioppino, Sonoma Seafood, 183
Clam, Chowder, Jeff's Christmas Eve, 174
Clam, Linguini in a Chardonnay Infused White Sauce, 30
Crab, Big Boy's Kunde Family, 180
Crab, Mini Cakes with Citrus Aioli, 161
Crab, Salad with Tangerines and Ruby Beets, 169
Crab, Wontons with Sesame Soy Dipping Sauce, 165
Fish, Sriracha Lime Grilled Tacos, 74
Halibut, with Fennel, Olives and Cherry Tomatoes, 79
Oysters, Half Shell with Magnolia Lane Mignonette, 8
Prawns, Mushroom Risotto with Saffron, 124
Salmon, Miso-Glazed with Shiitake Mushroom Rice, 123
Shrimp, Crostini with Fresh Dill, 12
Shrimp, Seafood Capellini Salad, 20

Soups

Curried Butternut Squash Soup, 120
Fresh Corn Chowder with Crispy Bacon, 73
Heirloom Tomato Soup with Parmesan Crostini, 119
Jeff's Christmas Eve Clam Chowder, 174
Penne and White Bean Soup with Italian Sausage and Fresh Spinach, 173
Pork Pozole, 177
Watermelon and Tomato Gazpacho, 65

Vegetables

Arugula, Fresh, Roasted Red Pepper Hamburger Pizza with Smoked Mozzarella, 87
Arugula, Salad, Grilled Peach with Feta and Spicy Seed Brittle, 69
Bean, Black, Festive Layered Dip, 62
Bean, Black, Smoky Chili, 188
Bean, White, Penne Soup with Italian Sausage and Fresh Spinach, 173
Beets, Ruby, Crab Salad with Tangerines, 169
Bok Choy, Beef Stir-Fry, Shiitake Mushrooms over Rice, 83
Brussel Sprout, Roasted, Salad with Apples, Bacon and Toasted Pecans, 170
Butternut Squash, Curried Soup, 120
Cabbage Slaw, Asian Chicken Wings with, 16
Cabbage, Napa, Chinese Chicken Salad with Toasted Sesame Seeds, 23
Cabbage, Savoy, Teriyaki Chicken and Scallions, 33
Chili, Green, Grilled Chicken with Corn, Salsa, 80
Corn, Chowder with Crispy Bacon, 73
Corn, Festive Layered Bean Dip, 62
Corn, Grilled Chicken and Green Chili Salsa, 80
Cucumber, Pork Satay Lettuce Wraps and Zesty Peanut Sauce, 38
Fava Bean, Fresh, Bruschetta, 15
Fennel, Halibut with Olives and Cherry Tomatoes, 79
Fennel, Maple Pork Chops with Caramelized Figs, 187

Green Bean, Salad with Baby Potatoes and Herb Dijon Vinaigrette, 70
Mushroom, Lasagna, Caramelized Onion and Béchamel Sauce, 130
Mushroom, Medley, Red Wine Infused Beef Stroganoff, 192
Mushroom, Risotto with Prawns and Saffron, 124
Mushroom, Shiitake, Beef Stir-Fry and Bok Choy over Rice, 83
Olive, Halibut with Fennel and Cherry Tomatoes, 79
Olive, Tapenade served with Baked Brie Cheese and Crostini, 11
Onion, Caramelized, Harvest Pear Crostini, 108
Onion, Caramelized, Grilled Rib Eye Steaks with Blue Cheese, 92
Onion, Caramelized, Lasagna with Mushrooms and Béchamel Sauce, 130
Pepper, Roasted Red, Hamburger Pizza with Smoked Mozzarella and Fresh Arugula, 87
Portobello, Grilled, Sandwich with Caramelized Onions, Pesto Mayo and Balsamic Glaze, 27
Potatoes, Baby, Green Bean Salad and Herb Dijon Vinaigrette, 70
Potatoes, Baby, Prosciutto Wrapped with a Dijon Drizzle, 166
Potatoes, Yukon Gold, Roasted Lemon Thyme Chicken, 133
Pumpkin, Chocolate Ricotta Cheesecake with a Chocolate Wafer Crust, 203
Spinach, Fresh, Penne and White Bean Soup with Italian Sausage, 173
Spinach, Strawberry Salad with Marcona Almonds, 66
Tomato, Cherry, Halibut with Fennel and Olives, 79
Tomato, Fresh Garden Bruschetta, 57
Tomato, Heirloom, Soup with Parmesan Crostini, 119
Tomato, Sun Dried, Melted Brie in Garlic Sourdough, 162
Tomato, Watermelon Gazpacho, 65